ADVENTURES OF A

PIPE TRAVELER

BY

DAVID W SENIK

Author's Note

This is my first book in a series of memoirs during my 40 years of traveling the United States. This particular book defines my quest in the search of fine pipes and tobaccos. On my Journey in semis, cars, boats and planes along with being involved in the specialized automotive transport, film industry, logging and oil fields, I encounter a vast array of eclectic individuals I have met along the way. My search for pipes and cigars, have opened many doors and many visits to Tobacconists throughout the country.

This is a compendium of events that I have experienced not a how to book but a number of encounters that still bring a smile to my face.

The reviews expressed in this book are mine. Some names have been changed to protect the guilty.

I hope you enjoy this book. Thank you for your purchase.

Pull up a chair and enjoy the journey!

David Senik

Table of Contents

Chapter I ......The Beginnings

Chapter II ......On the Road Again

Chapter III ......The Pacific Northwest

Chapter IV ......Logging

Chapter V ....East Coast

Chapter VI ......Back in the Mitten

Chapter VII ......Back On the Road Again

Chapter VIII ......Changes

Chapter IX......The Contest

Chapter X ......Autorama-Detroit

Chapter XI ......The Road Calls Again

Chapter XII ......How This Book Came to Be

CHAPTER I

THE BEGINNING

Chances are that if you are reading this you either enjoy a good smoke whether it is an exceptional bowl of fine pipe tobacco or a fine cigar, good for you. I would take my hat off to you if I wore one, but I don't, a hat is my basic idea of rain gear (more of that later). I've been in a search for exceptional tobacco for 30 years or more. Thinking back on this never ending journey I thought I would share some of my adventures with others in search of the same elusive quest for the perfect pipe tobacco or the one fine cigar that just seems to hit all the right notes.

I'd like to say that I've been a lifelong connoisseur of pipes but that is not the case here. I didn't start to fully appreciate a good pipe or the better tobacco's until I was in my mid 20's. That's not to say that I did not smoke before then I did like a damn chimney. Cigarettes were my primary smoke of choice for quite a few years, with the occasional drugstore cigar or pipe now and then. What I'm trying to explain here is I had no earthly clue as to what a good smoke was all about. That being said this is my personal journey in search of fine tobacco products. Thinking back on it, it's been a very interesting journey. So without further ado this is an account of my adventures as to the best that my feeble mind can remember.

I can't remember if I was 12 or 13 when I read THE ADVENTURE'S OF HUCKLBERRY FINN and TOM SAWYER I guess I was always destined to be a pipe smoker. Maybe it was the way in which MARK TWAIN described the virtues of smoking or the fact that a young adventures soul could take so much pleasure from a pipe that got to me, I can't really say. What I do know is that I must have read those books 2 or 3 dozen times. I've always had a curiosity to see and find out what was around the next bend or over the next hill. Growing up in HOWELL, Michigan there were quite a few likeminded kids in my section of town. We had a field that we played and built forts in called

FRENCHES FIELD, Which was owned by Mr. French who lived two doors down from me. Now to a bunch of youngsters with visions of Pirates, Marauders and all manner GI JOE type of characters we could mimic in that field, was a magical place indeed. I don't remember exactly how we managed to come in possession of a few corn cob pipes but we did. HUCK FINN I was. We tried to smoke just about everything we could dry up in and put in the bowls. Now across the street from the field was a ball park that everyone called Bruce Field. We would go over there and scout under the bleachers for cigar butts to crumple up and load up our pipe bowls. As I remember that was a lot better than leaves or grass. That being my introduction to smoking I have always been intrigued by pipes. I mean if it was good enough for MARK TWAIN there just had to be something with merit to it.

My grandfather had seven brothers and it seemed like I was always hanging around them and their friends. Some of these characters smoked a cigar or a pipe. There again if it was good enough for them so it had to be for me. Shortly after I started driving, I got a job working with my best friend Bob Garbin who was working for his uncle Gene at G & G Paint driving a delivery truck. Now this was a very cool thing to do. Getting paid to drive and being basically my own boss I knew I had found my calling. During that time I didn't smoke a pipe all that much but I was never without a corn cob pipe just in case I felt the need for a bowl. And so it was for quite a few years as I strived to advance and gain more experience in the trucking industry. I spent a few years hauling auto parts from the Midwest to assembly plants up and down the east coast in an 18 wheeler. After the bottom fell out of auto industry in the mid to late 70's I heard there was work to be had in Texas. So off I went in search of work and a new adventure. Now for a Yankee showing up in Texas was a real eye opener. Those people were still fighting the Civil war down there. I couldn't believe this crap. In my mind I thought hey, we won get over it.

For some reason I was under the impression there would be a lot of pipe and cigar smokers in the south. In certain parts it was true, but for the most part people in that neck of the woods indulged in mostly chewing tobacco the leaf Mail Pouch type but usually Skoal or something similar. Arriving in Houston I needed to make some money fast, as I was pretty much broke. Texas at this time was like a modern day boomtown, much like what Williston, North Dakota is now in 2013. I was hanging around the pool at the motel I was staying at and met a fellow pipe smoker who was taking a few days off from working on the oil rigs. Being a fellow pipe smoker we hit it off rather quick. He introduced himself as Wild Willy, top notch roughneck. Willy liked to smoke like a damn train; this guy was extremely serious about his tobacco. He would usually have a cigar or pipe in his mouth and a BIG wad of chewing tobacco in his cheek. We got to talking and started a friendship that would last for years. Now to simply call Willy a character would not do him justice at all, far from it, Old Willy stood about 6' 2" a black and gray crew cut and a beard that reached down to his chest. Without a doubt one of the most interesting people I would ever meet. We sat by the pool, smoked and had more than a few beers while I listened to him give me his take on all manner of tobacco, oil rigs on land and in the Gulf of Mexico. This all sounded very interesting to me, I sat there and soaked up all this info like a sponge. Willy was the foreman on an oil rig 100 hundred miles or so west of Houston. He said if I could work my tail off hard, stay with it and always think of safety for myself as well as those around me he would hire me as a roughneck. This all sounded great to me as it was hard work as well as interesting. So a couple days later I had my introduction to oil rigs. What a blast that was, 12 to 18 hour shifts working on the drilling platform was enjoyable to me as I've never backed down from a challenge involving hard work. Being raised with a strong work ethic didn't hurt either. The work was dirty, hard and very noisy, I loved it. The guys I worked with were some hard guys, from a wide variety of backgrounds. I don't really know why but I've always seemed to wind up being around such people. To me that's not bad thing at all, as I've met many interesting individuals throughout the years.

While on the platform you couldn't smoke as things were very flammable to say the least. Not only that but you were too busy to smoke anything while working. After our shift was done and we got cleaned up as best we could it was time to lite a fire and cook dinner. That usually consisted of throwing a grate of whatever we could take off the rig such as a protective grate from a belt housing or something, throw that over the fire and burn the oil and grease off it and you were ready to toss the spuds and steaks on. After dinner we would sit around the fire each of us smoking the tobacco of choice. Willy most always smoked a huge pipe. Me, I still smoked my trusty corn cob. Sitting there out on the vast expanse of west Texas one could lookout at what seemed like forever and see nothing but stars and the weather coming in. Thinking back it was a very enjoyable time. Sitting there smoking our pipes, cigars, and cigarettes you could hear the steady drone of the rig, once in a while we could hear the distant howl of a coyote or see a rabbit or some other critter scampering through the brush. I would sit there and listen to all the stories these guys would tell of rough necking, ranching, and construction work or whatever was the topic of the night. It was very unique to sit listening to the old grizzled hands talk; looking off in the distance you could see the lights of another oil rig. Being from Michigan where you couldn't see that far in any one direction this was great.

I worked seven days on two days off, which worked out well. My time off was spent hanging out with Willy, most of the time we went down to Galveston as Willy knew of a great tobacconist that carried everything tobacco. This place was almost magical walking through the door and was akin to stepping back in time. I do not remember exactly how long the shop had been there but I do recall the proprietor telling me that it had survived more than a few hurricanes. This is where I was introduced to a better grade of pipe than I had been smoking. At that time I was rough on pipes so having a real high end pipe at the time didn't make a whole lot of sense to me. Instead the owner of the shop proposed that starting off with higher end basket pipes would be my best way to go, as they would give me a better smoke than say tour a typical drug store pipe. So after loading up with enough tobacco products for Willy and myself and the rest of the rig crew it was time to have some fun.

Galveston is quite a unique place indeed, besides having a great pipe shop and fantastic places to eat there was water. During my first trip there with Willy he felt it was his duty to give me the grand tour of the island, and what a tour it turned out to be. There we were cruising around Galveston in Willy's 1970 ragtop Corvette. (Did I mention earlier that Willy was a Corvette guy too?) Anyway we were checking out the marinas, boats, the girls of course and just about anything else that drew our attention. We came upon the coolest beach that had an abundance of sun bathing babes that had a Tiki Bar food stand and a surf shop. I was in my element now. Of course we threw out the anchor and proceeded to check out this beach of many visions. Well, here we go, Willy and I after maybe 20 seconds of deep thoughtful deliberation decided the best course of action would be to enjoy our pipe and libation of choice at said Tiki Bar and ponder at all the wonderful sights before us. We sat for a bit watching the babes and the surf. I had done quite a bit of surfing while visiting my Uncle Jack in San Clemente, California in my teens so off to the surf shop I went. My new pipe was smoking quite well as I entered the shop, yes if you're wondering it was a bit of a strange sight to see a pipe smoking dude salivating over all the surfboards, I got more than a few weird looks. Did I care? Not in the least, after scoping out the boards I inquired to the surf dudes there what would be the best board for the type of waves there. After purchasing a new pair of swim trunks a half body wet suit surf leash and board I was ready to hit the waves. Back over to the Tiki Bar I informed Willy I was off to catch some waves. By this time Willy had started to entertain a few of the babes at the bar. He thought I was absolutely nuts. Yup that's me, certifiably nuts. People at the bar didn't think it would be such a good idea if I went out with pipe in mouth, I was thinking along the same lines. Think of Popeye in surf shorts, barefoot on a surfboard riding the waves that would be yours truly. I had a blast, it took a few sets for me to get my groove back but once I did the sets just kept on rolling in. After a couple hours surfing it was time to think about where to spend the rest of the night.

Willy had a cousin that had a shrimp boat in Kemah, Texas. So off we went in search of a shrimp dinner. We must have looked like an eclectic sight hauling ass down the road, the top down in a 1970 Corvette Big Block the side pipes just a howling, two guys puffing away on our pipes with a surf board sticking up in the air, life was good. Besides being a car fanatic I love boats, any kind of boats, but I must say that sailboats are my boat of choice. There is just something about harnessing the wind and working with your sails to get to where you want to go. That evening we hung out on the waterfront with Willy's cousin Dragger, I never did find out what Dragger's real name was. He was given that nick name on account of he didn't enjoy anything as much as dragging for oysters, drinking beer came in a close second though. And yes this guy was a real character too.

It didn't take long for word to get out that Wild Willy was on the dock, him being a bit of a celebrity on account of some of his wild antics around the water front. We started out in the bar/café on the docks. Soon we were getting too loud so we moved the gathering outside. What a meal we had, the fishermen brought some great shrimp, oysters, and all kinds of fish. Into a huge pot it all went along with some other ingredients of questionable varieties. The party was on. Everyone had a grand time as after dinner we sat around the shrimp boats and listened to the fishermen spin there yarns. Now being watermen, pipe smoking prevailed. It was interesting to observe all the different types of pipes these salty guys were smoking. Seeing as how this was a kicked back affair basically on land most everyone smoked their sitting pipes. These ranged from large briars to huge long meerschaums. What was interesting to me was the wide variety of carvings on these unique white pipes. I started asking about these works of art. Finding out that they came from a sea cru station in a faraway foreign land was more than cool in my mind. Now all of these folks were real characters. Just the kind of people I find entertaining. The following day Willy and I went with Dragger shrimping out in the bay. What an interesting experience that was. We had some very unusual marine life get caught up in the nets. I found out what gave the meal the night before the tastes of questionable repute. Hey, it was all good to me. That is where I developed a keen appreciation for all manner of sea food. If it comes out of the water I'll eat it. Food I would find out in the coming years was much like tobacco. One must acquire a taste for some things but others taste great the first time you put it in your mouth.

After we unloaded the boat that day we had another fine dinner, then we headed back to the rig, ready to search for oil the next day. And so it went pretty much like that for the next few months. I did a lot of shrimping during that time. As at least one of my days off, I would go back down to Kenah and crew on one of the shrimp boats. This was a plus for myself and also the owners of the boats as they got a crew member that worked hard and was free, besides, I got to learn a lot about working boats, tides, commercial fishing and had a blast. There was one crusty old salt of a fisherman that had the coolest looking old wooden bay shrimp boat. This old timer smoked a very different type of blend he made up himself, what made this concoction so different was that while smoking it you would get a whiff of it and smell something like fried oysters, or something to do with the sea. Kicked back on our way back in one day, I asked Chan what the hell was in that bowl, he looked over at me with that wise old amusing twinkle in his eyes and said, well I'll tell ya but don't let my secret out as I've got enough nicknames I don't care to have any more attached to my person.

Oh sure Chan I would never think about divulging your secret blend, cross my heart and all that, I said.

This blend has taken me many, many, years and a considerable amount of thought and deep contemplation for me to come up with just the right amount of all the different components, to arrive at this perfect smoke which I've been enjoying for over some 27 years.

Come on Chan, do tell! Judging by the gleam in his eyes, I knew this was going to be one hell of a good story.

One thing you need to understand is that Chan has been a waterman for his entire life, he was in his 60's, when I met him.

Well Dave, this is how this sea blend is made. I take some Carter Hall, Holiday, and black Cavendish, a good dose of perique a dash of latakikea and some seaweed, I gather from the back of the oyster dredge, that all gets blended together, wrapped up in an old fish bait rag, then pressed as best as can be, then put in the forecastle just above the bilge and there it matures for about eight months to a year. Sounds like a real bastard of a mix right? Well, let me tell you, Chan gave me a couple ounces to try and that stuff turned out to be one of the most finally tuned blends I've ever smoked. I know it sounds a bit peculiar to say the least but this was good stuff, especially if you liked the aroma and taste of the sea. To say this concoction was different would be a gross understatement. Overall it was very deep with a musty type quality to it. But then there were hints of the latakea and stronger notes of perique the taste of the seaweed was very present, but it all came together with a nice flavor. I've never had anything quite like it since then and I don't imagine I ever will. But isn't that why we are always willing to go out on a limb and try knew blends or new pipes?

After a few months of drilling holes in west Texas some of the guys including myself got the opportunity to work off shore in the Gulf of Mexico. This to me was something I couldn't pass up, and so after taking a week off to surf and go shrimping with the watermen. We went to a school to learn the ins and outs of working off shore. The first offshore rig I worked on located some 100 plus miles from shore were great. All there is out there is you the rig and the sea as far as the eye could see. Off duty time was spent in the R & R space or leaning on a rail looking out over the gulf smoking your pipe. Being out in the gulf pipes were the smoke of choice. What made it majestic at night was to look out and see other rigs working off in the distance with their lights blazing. Now and then you could see a work boat coming out to supply one of the rigs with pipe, food or whatever was needed on the platform. This went on for a few months. Then Willy got a job offer up in Alaska, I could have gone there with him but the road was calling my name once again.

CHAPTER II

ON THE ROAD AGAIN

While I was working on land in West Texas we most usually got our pipe delivered to us by a first class oil field hauling company called Ray Bellew & Sons. Their motto was they could move the world if they had a place to put it. These rigs were nice. The finest, best looking trucks I had ever seen. Showing up on their doorstep one morning I filled out an application and was fortunate to get hired as I didn't have any oil field hauling experience but I did know my way around an oilrig. And so it was, Willy went to the Great Tundra of Alaska and I went to work in the oil patch in a different capacity.

Most of what we hauled was all sorts of pipe for the rigs. During this time holes were being drilled everywhere. Basically we hauled to the states surrounding Texas with an occasional run to the oil fields in the north. While working at Bellew & Sons I met a few other pipe smokers. These guys were a helpful bunch as they took me under their wing and taught me the ropes, as I had loaded flatbed trailers before but never pipe. Besides pipe we would haul anything oil rig related. Such as well heads machinery etc. After getting the hang of what I was doing it started to be fun, I enjoyed the challenge of loading and unloading the proper way. Most of our loads went directly to the oil rigs wherever they might be. Once at the rig you would pull your trailer within inches of the pipe racks and unload your pipe bye yourself this was dangerous to say the least but done properly with a sharp eye out for what could go drastically wrong and seriously mess you up if not kill you, this to me was great fun indeed. If you were lucky once in a while there would be a front end loader that could unload the pipe for you. Those rigs were few and far between, usually the bigger platforms for Exxon or one of the other big oil companies.

A lot of our runs would go to Odessa, Texas. The company headquarters were in Houston and we used to load our pipe or whatever, and haul ass out to west Texas, unload, find a phone in the middle of nowhere call dispatch to see if there was a backhaul to be picked up someplace and if there wasn't you would drop the hammer and get back to Houston an do it all over again. We were paid on a percentage basis so the more you could haul the more money you would make. During this time there was no such thing as how much things cost in the oil field, it was how soon it could get there.

I had considered myself to be a hard runner. Meaning one that was capable of running your ass off until you arrived at whatever destination the load needed to go. Man, was I in for a surprise, these guys could run and I do mean run hard. I was used to opening the trailer doors backing into a dock and watching some overweight slug on a forklift load my trailer at his convenience. Having to chain down a load making sure it was secure and not going to shift in any way jump in the cab, and drive 600 to 800 hundred miles was a totally different story. Needless to say I had a lot to learn. Once again I was the odd man out especially being a Yankee. I could never to this day figure out what the big deal was about being a Yankee. Years earlier while my uncle Virgil was teaching me how to drive the big rigs I was given a great piece of advice. He told me that no matter where I was or what I was doing, always seek out and pay strict attention to the old guys. They are the ones that wrote the book on whatever we were doing. I on the other hand was just coming along and if I was lucky they would allow me to read it. I've always followed that advice and it has served me very well throughout the years to this day. Now these old timers were in there 60's and 70's at the time and most of them smoked a pipe so I basically fit right in. I very much enjoyed hearing about the crazy exploits they had. They kept me from getting seriously hurt while in the oil industry.

Running as long and hard as we did to get supplies to the rigs one would have to reach down deep inside oneself to get the job done in a fashion that was expected of you. One old timer in particular, everyone called him Smoke Stack (Hank) and I got along pretty well. Old Stack could load his truck fill a couple of thermoses and drive nonstop out to West Texas. I asked him how in the world he did this. He told me it all had to do with the type of tobacco he smoked.

Come on Stack give me a break you can't run like that by just puffing away on your pipe, I said. Stack could have been Robert Duvals twin brother in the movie Lonesome Dove, right from the cowboy boots to the hat. Besides that he had the same type of personality, and just about the same outlook on most everything.

Sure you can he tells me. One day we had some time to kill, as we waited for some other drivers to get back to the yard to pick up their paperwork so we could all run out west together. Stack took me to his favorite tobacco shop not too far from our yard. Stepping into this shop you could tell it had been there for quite some time. The walls were full of pipe displays of the usual brands plus they had cases everywhere filled with higher end pipes. One whole wall was dedicated to nothing but pipe tobacco, with about a quarter of it filled with more varieties of chewing tobacco than I ever would have imagined existed. I just kind of stood there with my mouth hanging open. What a place, Old Stack proceeded to order up different types of the better blended tobaccos for the both of us. While there I purchased a couple more pipes. Of course being there with Stack I had to get several different blends of Chew and Skoal type of smokeless tobacco. He informed me I had to purge myself of the Yankee ways that have corrupted me so far in my young life. I thought why not, when in Rome and all that. Stack proceeded to let me know I had to look and act the part of a westerner if I was going to fit in. Always one to embark upon something new I was all for it, lead on my friend I said. Now I needed pouches to put all this tobacco in besides containers to store the stuff that wouldn't fit in the pouches. Then came the cigars, you have to have a wide assortment of stogies on hand as I was informed that having extra to hand out to others I would meet in my travels was the polite and honorable way of conducting oneself. After all Stack said it just wasn't right to smoke anything or chew anything in front of someone without offering them whatever you were enjoying in front of them. This advice would serve me well, just as well then as it does now some 35 plus years later.

On the way back to the yard we stopped at a western wear store so I could get a pair of proper boots. Stack said that walking around in Yankee style boots was in extremely bad form. At first I wasn't too sure about this but after a bit of thought I came to the conclusion that I was the only driver around that wore square toed style Durango type boots. According to Stack and some of the other drivers, this would have to change. So into the store we go, I wasn't too sure about this pointy toed boot thing, but after trying a few pairs on they didn't seem too bad. They said that with a real cowboy boot you should be able to crush a cockroach in a corner. That was 35 years ago and I refuse to wear anything but to this day.

Getting back to all this new tobacco I purchased. Back in the drivers room at the yard Stack proceeded to coach me on what type of tobacco to blend with what others to come up with some blends that turned out to be very good. So from then on instead of smoking one cigarette after another while driving all night or most of the night I'd puff away on me pipes. It made the miles go by quicker and was more soothing than cigarettes. Stack told me that it was all about the journey, enjoy it, be one with your rig, be in tune you the truck your load and the road all jell together as one. From then on I slowed down a bit and started to be in a more relaxed, state of awareness. I wasn't as tired at the end of run either.

One night in particular I was going through some small towns on my way to a rig out near Odessa with some pipe. Below the pipe I had loaded a full load of 3 inch thick plate steel that went to a company in Midland, Texas that made the pumping rigs that pumped the oil out of the wells. Now I had in reality two complete loads on my trailer. Instead of grossing 80 thousand pounds I figured I was grossing around 110 thousand, only 30 thousand overweight. Now you must understand that back in that time hauling that kind of weight was pretty much the norm especially if one wanted to make money and stay in the good graces of the dispatchers. Some of you reading this might balk at this; I never said I was a saint now did I. So there I was strolling through this one town obeying every speed limit posted and out of nowhere comes this wieghmaster with lights just a flashing. Well shit, this is going to really suck. The boss did NOT like the drivers to get caught with loads like this even though we did it damn near every day.

The cop who pulled me over strolls up to the driver's side door, I put my pipe on the dash. While walking up to my cab I can see him giving my load a close look. This might not turn out so good I'm thinking, there's an oil rig that needs this pipe, besides the company in Midland expects this truck to be there when they open in the morning. Well there stands this lawman who looks like he just stepped out of a John Wayne movie. And just what the hell do you think you're doing coming through my town with this load; he said. Just going to a rig to get my pipe, jerk off, I tell him. By this time he had stepped up on my running board. Now anyone with half a brain could look at my tires and see how the trailer resembled a banana that I was beyond just pushing the limit by considerably more than a little. There he stands looking back at the load and checking me and the inside of my cab out then he eye balls my pipe on the dash. At this moment he's not saying a word. I figured here we go I wonder how this is going to turn out! That pipe still lit he asked? Should be I Said; just put it up there when you pulled me over. He gives me this look of mischievous amusement on his mug. Bring all your paperwork and your bills of lading back to my cruiser. Bring that pipe with you, DO NOT DUMP OUT WHATEVER IS IN IT!

Oh boy here we go this might not turn out so good, I'm thinking. Gathering up the registration, insurance, and the bills, I grabbed my pipe and go back to his cruiser. Climbing in the passenger seat I see Whyte Earp sitting there with a pipe stuck in the side of his mouth. Well looky here, just maybe this might turn out a little better than I had first anticipated. So I hand over all my paperwork. With not much more than a mere glance at my driver's license, registration, etc. he takes a long gander at my bills. Are you shitting me he said? Says here you've got 49 thousand pounds of pipe on and another 45 thousand pounds plate Steele under that. Just who in the hell do you think you are trying to run through my town with that kind of weight, the way I figure, your about 50 thousand pounds overweight! Gee officer I just haul what dispatch tells me to haul I picked it all up at our yard in Houston. I know exactly where your yard is. I've been there and talked to the man himself (Ray Bellew) about you cowboy's running through my town overweight and hauling ass with the hammer down. Oh no, not me I tell him, always obey the speed limits running through any town, the last thing you want to hear at night is a loud truck barreling through town.

He thought that statement to be pretty funny. Sitting there laughing and shaking his head he tells me that normally he'd have me follow him to the local grain elevator and weigh my truck. Being that you could only legally gross out at 80 thousand pounds, this could be a very big ticket, let alone the fact that he could require that I got the truck down to a legal limit before letting yours truly be on my merry way. He gives me this serious look and informs me that if I were to roll across the local elevator scale there was more than a good chance I would break said scale. So what do you suppose I should do with you young man? Well, that's totally up to you sir. I'm trying to be as polite as can be. Normally I would rake your ass over the coals carrying that much weight. The way I figure you are in a shit load of trouble, you know what I can make you do don't you? How about we go down to the café and you can make some calls and get half that load off. What you are trying to do is extremely dangerous, what if you had to stop in hurry? Well, I didn't have any problems getting out of Houston in stop and go traffic and as you observed for yourself there wasn't a problem with me stopping when your lights came on behind me. Then out of the blue he asked me what I was smoking in my pipe. Oh, it's a special blend my friend Smoke Stack mixed up for me, I tell him. Is that so? Follow me to the café. Stay off the radio (CB) you got some things to make right. Walking back to the cab I'm thinking, damn, the last thing I want to do is call dispatch this late at night and tell them I got caught. Especially since Ray himself would most likely answer the phone.

At the café I set the brakes, climb out of the cab, and walked up to Whyte Earp. He slowly crawls out and says, lets you and me step inside and talk this over a cup of coffee. Grab your pipe and that entire bag of special blend you assume is legal. What the hell is this crazy lawman thinking he's going to lock me up for smoking a pipe? Back to the truck I go. There was about a pound of this blend of tobacco in the sleeper, so grabbing that, I went back into the café where Whyte and the waitress are having a conversation at the counter. Let us sit in a booth he says. So we sit down and he introduces me to the waitress and tells me his name which I had already seen on his uniform shirt. Then he tells me with a grin on his face that in order to get out of the predicament I was in that maybe I should consider turning over my bag of contraband tobacco. While sitting there thinking of all the bad shit that's coming down upon me and thinking what the hell, this tobacco is LEGAL. You realize this particular blend cannot be purchased in the store. Meaning he informed me that one could not just waltz into a store and purchase it. Sure you can, I tell him. Out of the corner of my eye I could see the waitress standing behind the counter with an amused grin on her face clearly enjoying this conversation. Not true, says I, my friend Smoke Stack and I bought a bunch of tobacco in Houston and mixed it up at the yard. So, you admit this is a strange blend do you, something that must be mixed. Well what the hell, here I am sitting across from Whyte Earp 50 thousand pounds overweight, my log book hasn't been touched in days, wondering how I'm going to explain all this to the boss, let alone the fact that there's a whole crew on an oil rig waiting for pipe so they can keep on drilling. Well that's true, no you can't just walk in and buy this blend because it's made special.

At about that time I start to figure out these two are having a good time at my expense. Which could very well turn out to be costly to me and the company. Just then the waitress sets down two cups of coffee and informs me with a wink that this might take a while. The way I see it, there's one of several ways we could proceed from here as we have a very delicate situation here, Whyte informs me. Starting to get the jest of the predicament at hand I enquire as to what he thinks the best way would be to resolve these problems. Well, seeing as how this is such a major offence. The best thing for you to do is to relinquish that there bag of contraband so I can put it in my pipe, and then there won't be any evidence that way I could be inclined to possibly over look your other discrepancies. With that said, he and the waitress had a good laugh. They proceeded to inform me that my good friend Stack knew the both of them and just about everyone else in town. Wyatt, the waitress and Stack had all grown up together in the next town over and that Stack had called ahead and informed Karen the waitress that I was coming through with a heavy load and that if officer Pete wanted some of the tobacco that Stack made up for Pete the cop, this would be an excellent opportunity for all party's concerned to have a good laugh at my expense. Needless to say I gave most of my tobacco to Pete the coffee was on the house. The rig that was waiting on the pipe was only about 60 miles away right in the middle of nowhere of course. Pete turned out to be a colorful character indeed. He had a CB in the cruiser, after looking at the address of where the rig was he said I would most likely get lost and as we had spent a lot of time talking to put my radio on channel 2 and to follow him, he would lead me right there, just don't run over me with that heavy load I was told.

That was one of my introductions to the brotherhood of real pipe smokers. I would not trade that experience for the world. Back then Texas was still mostly like the old west in a lot of ways. Some laws were a bit lax. The bottom line being the oil industry needed some rules to be bent now and then. Being there in that era and time was a real blast. We all ran our ass off, working as hard as we could and when we had time off we played just as hard.

Pete and Karen and I became good friends. I never went through their town without stopping, enjoying a pipe full with Pete at the café. Although after that I did try and pull loads that were not so obviously overweight, what can I say, times were different back then.

I've always loved driving, especially trucks. Not just any truck mind you. Whatever truck I was driving at the time, I worked hard to make my equipment shine like a new nickel fresh out of the mint. That's how I was raised, whatever you drove it must be clean, waxed, and everything just so. And to drive nice equipment and be paid to drive and smoke my pipe, cigar or whatever was great. How many people can say that they love their job and look forward to doing it every day? Being a professional in the transportation industry has always been a good life for me, granted it's definitely not for everyone. It sure seems like we were all put on this earth to do something whatever it is you do. Some folks absolutely enjoy what they do and some not so much. I happen to be a soul with a wanderlust spirit deep inside me that knows no bounds. Traveling and seeing new places, meeting new and interesting people has been an adventure for me, one that I truly enjoy to this day.

After working in the oil industry for a year or so I was sent up to the Pacific Northwest with a load of drill pipe. Wow, what a place that country was, it took my breath away, the mountains, trees, crystal clear rivers you could see all the way to the bottom. I fell in love with that part of the country. There were lumber yards and saw mills everywhere. This I thought was the place for me.

CHAPTER III

THE PACIFIC NORTHWEST

After picking up a return load of machinery going to Dallas, I headed to Houston, packed up my belongings into my trusty pickup, said my goodbyes to my friends and coworkers and headed to Oregon.

Having a specific destination in mind was all well and good, but as it always should be, this adventure was more about the journey. As one of my favorite authors BOB BITCHIN (ROBERT LIPKIN) of Latitudes & Attitudes magazine fame and presently owner and publisher of CRUISING OUTPOST always stresses, the difference between adventure and misadventure is attitude. That being said, off I went in search of a new adventure. Having that mindset I decided to stick to the back roads as much as possible. The interstate system in the U.S.A. is a fantastic way to get around the country but in the same breath it has made it possible to drive from one shining sea to the other shining sea and not see much of anything. Some of my fellow drivers would say you don't see a damn thing, but that's their opinion. One can always find something interesting to see if only you wish to look hard enough. Having an eye out for the wonderful sights this great land of ours offers helps also. One thing I've noticed in all my years of travel and have driven well over 8 million miles is that a lot of folks just look straight ahead; some of these people don't even look in the mirror. Must get awful boring strolling down the road with blinders on? Now that I think about it, that's how a number of people go through life, to be that way or being normal scares the shit out of me. Anyway I'm getting ahead of myself here.

Ok back on track, heading out of Houston I thought it would be interesting to go through NEW MEXICO, UTAH, NEVADA, NORTHERN CALIFORNIA, then into OREGON. Where I would wind up I had a fair idea but mostly it was just a general place on the map. With a free spirit and gas in the tank and many miles to enjoy the journey, off I went. Staying on the back roads and not being in a hurry at all was great. Whenever I went through a little berg that looked even half way interesting I would stop and talk to the locals. If there happened to be a tobacco shop in town so much the better. I spent many an hour sitting on main streets of more than a few towns listening to the folks talk about their life and the history of the area.

Traveling through Utah my water pump went tits up, so after hitching a ride into town that wasn't really a town but more like a place on a lonely stretch of road, I went to this old time gas station that gave me the impression of being stuck in a time warp. The people there could not have been more helpful, as luck would have it the old timer in the garage working on an old Diamond Reo stake truck smoking a pipe that looked to be as old as he was, held together with what looked like some type of orange tape.

Knowing that with all the commotion that was not going on around there he had most likely seen me walking towards his shop for a while, as the main street I was walking down seemed to be empty of people, but there were a few dogs that just had to come up and check out the new stranger in town .

As my new found four legged friends and I walked onto the property I tried to read the sign atop the structure. This sign had to be about 60 years old, I could just barely make out Claytons Fuel & Repair, and the pumps said Sinclair Gas. Now there had been a Sinclair station in my home town in Howell, Michigan that had a good reputation for great repair service. There being a bench out front by the road I took a seat and played with the dogs for bit, walking into the garage area the guy working on the truck puts his wrench down, gives me the ounce over and asks, going far young man? Yup, going up to Oregon, I tell him.

He stands there takes his cap off, puffs on his pipe a time or two and say's, damn boy that's a bit far to walk all that way aint it?

Not walking I say, the water pump in my all of a sudden not so trusty pickup truck took a shit on me, just about 15 miles south of town.

Well he says, could be worse. Could have blown the engine or lost your transmission or something like that. Then you'd be in a bigger fix, look at the bright side. Where ya coming from anyway, don't believe I've seen you around here before and I know every person within 50 miles of town.

I'm coming out of Houston Texas, on my way to the Northwest looking for work. But it seems like I'll be here till I can find a pump. You wouldn't happen to have an auto parts store here? He's standing there deep in thought and knowing by the vibes I'm getting that nothing around this town is going to happen in any kind of hurry. I pull out one of my beat up old pipes in my pouch and start filling it. All the while I'm doing this he's standing there watching me load my pipe.

After lighting my pipe he introduced himself as Matt Flanagan fixer of all things fixable and sole proprietor of Claytons Fuel & Repair. Pleased to meet you, David Senik is my name, I tell him while shaking his outstretched hand. We sat on the bench talking for a time, soaking up the afternoon sun. To a normal person this might be an inconvenience, not so with me, as Matt I could tell right off the bat, was quite the character. Picture a thin version of Wilford Brimley with a pipe and wearing a ball cap. With that same type of demeanor and speech, that would be Matt.

No Dave, he says we don't have a parts store here. Nearest one is 70 miles away. There's a junkyard not too far out of town might have one though. I need to get that old Reo done for a customer, after that we'll see what can be done for ya.

Great, sounds good to me, I'm rather worried about my truck sitting down the road as there isn't a cap on it, and all my stuff is right out in the open inside the bed.

Oh, not a problem, Joe's over at the diner, lets you and I hop on over.

And who might Joe be I asked, as we set off with about a half dozen dogs trailing us.

He's our constable, if he's not too involved with anything besides maybe a slice of pie, which he doesn't need, I'll get him to go keep an eye on your rig till we can get it back here.

Joe turned out to be a pleasant man. He wasn't eating pie but looked as if he didn't miss too many meals either. Sure he'd be glad to head out there and keep an eye on my truck, might even capture a speed demon while I'm there, he says with a wink. I knew my truck was safe.

After getting that taken care of back to the shop we go with dogs in tow. I asked Matt if I could help get the old REO running.

Why would you want to work on that old thing for me, he asked?

Are you kidding I say, that's a real antique, what year is that. I've never laid eyes on anything like that.

It's a 1948 Diamond Reo with a flat head in it. Gotta put a radiator in it that wasn't made for it, as you can guess that's a hard item to find and I need to do a little fabricating to make the new one fit.

No sweat Matt, I'd be glad to help. So the rest of the afternoon we spent cutting this, welding that, fitting this hose and everything else needed to complete the job and by six o'clock in the evening it was done. It was a joy working on that old truck.

Looking around while working on the Reo I hadn't seen any type of repair or tow truck, but there was an old pole barn type building in back of the station.

Matt waved for me to follow him and headed off towards the barn. After pulling back this huge door there sat an old Auto Car

Tow Truck. This thing was far out. It looked like almost new. Painted that old auto car green with pin striping on it, Matt said it was a 1954 with an updated 290 Cummins engine, twin stick transmissions. It had started out life as a long haul road tractor he got it cheap about 10 years before and had spent two years rebuilding it in what spare time he had. This truck was nothing short of kewl man. It had an integrated sleeper on it with a half-moon window, old style Dayton shoed wheels, twin chrome stacks, and purred like a fine tuned sewing machine. I was all over this truck, this thing was spotless. To see an auto car of that vintage in the middle of the desert was a sight indeed. While I was gawking all over it, on top and under it, I automatically just had to lift up the hood flaps and check out the horse (Engine), while under there I checked the oil (clean), and all other fluids.

Matt stood there just like a proud father puffing away on his taped up pipe.

After a spell he shakes his head, looks at me and says, never seen anybody besides himself get so excited over an old truck.

Old I say, this even smells new, I told him that back in Michigan we pulled a lot of weight and that auto cars were some of the work horses of choice and that I used to work for a guy in Cinnaminson, New Jersey who had a couple of these in his shop and his son wanted to restore them. I told him whenever I was there servicing my truck I could stare at them forever and just imagine the stories they could tell.

Matt then asked if I had ever driven a two stick.

Oh yeah, been operating more 2 sticks than single.

Jump in you drive. So off we went. Now you must understand this was an old time truck, you actually had to work to operate it. No power steering or any of the modern equipment we take for granted these days. We got to my pickup and sure enough Joe was still there watching over it. After towing it back to the garage it was late, there being no motel in town Matt said I could sleep in the tow truck. The next morning we went to the recycle parts yard and found a pump off another 302 Ford engine that matched mine just right.

After putting on the replacement pump, I thanked Matt and Joe and was on my way again. Any chance I got while trucking through Utah I'd stop in to visit with Matt and Joe, of course the dogs too.

Sticking to the back roads, taking my time worked out well. I would drive till an hour or so before dusk, find a roadside park next to some water like a river, lake, or stream. Back in those days you didn't have to worry so much about evil doers as one does these days. I would drop the tailgate, set up the portable grill, toss some meat on, have dinner and usually talk with other travelers doing pretty much the same thing as I was.

Getting into northern California was great as the mountains were getting bigger and the trees were doing the same and there were more of them. Continuing north to Oregon I somehow wound up near Monroe, OR where I met Dick Grace, he was a retired cat skinner (bulldozer operator) building logging roads and a logger. Dick turned out to be quite a knowledgeable person about all things logging, lumber, mountains, and just about anything else related to the Pacific Northwest.

Dick didn't smoke a pipe but he loved chewing tobacco of all types. He and his wife Mary lived on the side of a mountain west of town, with a great view of a huge valley. Dick had this horse, an Arabian Stud Horse named Shae. This horse loved tobacco as much as Dick did. If you had a cigar or any type tobacco in your shirt pocket he would try and get it from you. Whenever I visited Dick I would always pick up a few pouches of chew and some cheap cigars for Shae. He wasn't picky either he would eat all things tobacco. Didn`t matter what, menthol cigarettes, snuff, whatever, he would munch it up. Dick said he never had to worry about worming him. I've never seen an animal before or since that would eat tobacco like Shae would. Good thing he wasn't my horse I could see where his habits could get expensive. Dick didn't mind, he loved that horse.

Dick took the time to show me the lay of the land seeing as I was what he referred to as a flatlander I needed to know some things about the mountains. This country was very much like something out of a movie set only better, it was the real thing. He took me up to a lot of the logging roads he had helped to build. We would also visit some logging camps that were way cut in the hills. I had no idea people even did this anymore. Think AX MEN, the TV show only this was back in the early 80's. After I got a feel for the country it was time to find work. I had looked for work around Eugene, OR but not having any mountain experience I didn't have much luck. Having heard that trucking companies in Roseburg, Oregon were hiring, I headed there Roseburg being about a hundred miles south right off of I-5.

After arriving in Roseburg I spent a few days checking it and the surrounding areas out. After that I took a drive over to the coast. Coos Bay was due west only 80 miles. That turned out to be an interesting city with a lot of fishing, commercial ship traffic, and quite a few saw mills, both big mills such as Weyerhaeuser, Boise Cascade plus the smaller family owned mills. I wanted to stay and work out of the coast but after a few days I called a company in Sutherland, Oregon I had put in application in the week before and got hired on there. So, after finding a place to rent there, I was back on the road again.

This outfit was not exactly the best trucking outfit in the area but was a good place to learn. We covered 17 Western States. We would haul lumber products out and all manner of loads back to Oregon or Washington State. This part of the country was fantastic; I fell in love with it and the people there. Everything seemed to be so much bigger there.

Humidity and I have never gotten along very well at all. Out there it was a dry climate. Texas was a humid sonofabitch. After being down there, then coming to the northwest was heaven to me. It didn't take me too long to get used to the terrain out there or the seasons. I just took my time, enjoyed my pipes and had a good time. Every trip was a new adventure. It didn't take me long to find a tobacconist after arriving in the area. On a side street not far from downtown Roseburg on the south side of town. I cannot remember the name of this shop, what I do remember is that it had a fine selection of pipes, pipe tobacco, cigars, and any type of smokeless tobacco one could imagine.

After working for that company for about a year, it was time to move up to a better class of outfit. There was a company in Roseburg called Terrain Tamers, now they had some nice equipment and paid a lot more than I was earning. I got to know some of the drivers that worked there and started to bug them to see if they could get me hired there. Douglas County was a close nit area at the time and it didn't take me long to get a reputation for keeping my equipment in top form. That was my ace in the hole getting hired there. When I started there they only had one truck available, it was a 1982 cab over (flat front, no hood) Freightliner. Nobody there wanted to drive it as it had no power steering, no air ride, and for being only not quite a year old looked to be in rough shape, nobody liked the color either, it was turquoise. I mean it was all turquoise, the frame on the truck and trailer, even the axels, the flatbeds were white, and it had nice aluminum wheels all the way around. To me this truck showed potential. It didn't take me long to turn that truck into quite the show piece. Strolling all over the western part of the country with such a truck was great. I took a lot of pride in my ride. I remember one trip where I had picked up a load of kiln dried clear (meaning no knots) cedar planking. It was going to a ski lodge in Snowmass, Colorado I had stopped in Bend, Oregon to fuel, eat and fill my thermos with super strong coffee, (I like it rich and strong) it was between dusk and dark. Cruising east of Brothers, Oregon I had just filled my pipe and lit it, got it going real good and out of nowhere a Great Horned Owl flew right in front of my windshield. Scared the shit right out of me, this bird was huge; the wing span had to be eight feet if it was an inch. Needless to say, my pipe flew out of my mouth, bounced off the steering wheel onto my lap with burning embers everywhere.

With trying to keep the truck on this old two lane road and trying to put the embers on my pants out, this was starting to get a bit interesting. I had heard about these huge Owls but had never laid eyes on one. Finally getting things back under control, I just sat there in awe for a few minutes while my mind processed what had just happened. After a few miles I looked around at all the tobacco that spilled all over the cab and started laughing my ass off. I wonder who was more startled me or the owl. That was a very majestic looking bird.

One other time it was late fall an after delivering lumber in Reno, NV I had traveled east on I-80 to US 447 north to a gypsum plant in Gerlach, Nevada about 120 miles north of I-80. Now when I say this place was in the middle of nowhere I mean it, look it up. The load I picked up went to some place in Oregon so I had the choice of taking the longer safer way back or taking a shortcut notorious for being a rough way to go. By now you know me well enough to guess what route I took. Yup, the back way, north for a while then over to California then into Oregon. This way had a mountain on it about 30 miles north of Gerlach. This grade was famous for tearing up transmissions, drive shafts, and rear ends. It was a difficult grade as there was a sharp right curve just before you started up the mountain that if you were to take too fast you stood a good chance of shifting your load if not flipping over on your side. That night was a full moon, no clouds, and nice crisp cool dry air. The driver's side window was open. I had just lit my pipe a few miles back and had just completed the right curve and was dropping 2 and 3 gears at time as this was about a 10% grade, on my left was a ravine on my right was the side of the mountain in which I was starting to climb. All of a sudden I caught movement out of my left eye, starting to turn my head right to see if anything was there, up out of the ravine comes this big black horse. It comes up onto the road and is running right next to me, having the window down I was looking him right in the eye, what a sight. I spun my head back forward then quickly back to the right, my pipe fly's out of my mouth bounces off the horses back, he gets more spooked than he already is, bolts forward cuts in front of me and the truck, then scales the side of the mountain on the right. WOW what a sight, you need to understand that I was only going about 10 to 15 M.P.H. at the time. Shit, a wild mustang, what a beautiful animal in his natural environment I lost a good pipe but having the chance to see such a sight right next to me was well worth it. To this day I think back on that night as if it was yesterday. Every time I think about it I grin shake my head and chuckle a bit. Trucking around out in the west were some of the most memorable times of my life. I had met a few other pipe smokers on the road and every now and then we'd run across each other.

Running into southern California was a regular run. After unloading in the Los Angeles Basin, if there wasn't a load to pick up that day I would go out to Ontario, California to the 76 Truck Stops. There were two of them there on the Southside of the I-10 just 5 miles away from the Fontana Speedway. Back then the speedway wasn't even there yet. I think they still used the Speedway in Riverside at the time. I could be wrong though as my memory fails me at times. Saying that Ontario was wild would be a gross understatement. You could get anything you wanted there and some things you didn't want. Every driver that unloaded in the Los Angeles area were waiting for back hauls, or were waiting to unload soon, would spend the night there then as it is now, one had to get there early or the lots would be full. That place was just a big party at both locations.

After getting my truck washed if needed, I would park and grab a coke or two, get something to take back to the truck to eat, kick back and enjoy the show for the night. I would sit there catching up on paperwork and clean the truck while smoking my pipe. During this time more and more trucks would be coming in for the night. Picture damn near every long haul truck in a 90 mile radiace all trying to get into these two joints. I always got a kick out of watching the different trucks from all over the country. Sitting, enjoying my pipe, I would look at the different trucks, and observe them as they tried to figure out where they wanted to park. Back then trucks had character, they were all different, hell in those days the whole country still had character. Watching the different styles of trucks coming in I could almost always tell what state they were from, at the least what section of the United States. It seemed as though each truck had its own personality, kind of like every pipe is a pipe but each one with its individuality. The same could be said of drivers of that era. Not so anymore as you look at trucks today, they all look like cookie cutter trucks; besides color they all give the impression of coming out of the same mold that holds true with the folks who drive them too. Unless you happen to be from the old school or are one of a dying breed of the elite that roam the highways and byways of this nation, everything looks just plain old plain. I'll discuss this further on, it will be fun.

One time in particular was more interesting than most. I had pulled in and parked early one day. It was a fairly hot afternoon, having finished doing paperwork. Eating, and wiping down my rig, I settled in my seat and started to enjoy my pipe. For some reason to this day I've never been able to figure out how drivers would park; drop their trailer and bobtail around the parking lot in both truck stops. This could get entertaining as the evening progressed, the CB radio was just ablaze with people trying to buy or sell just about anything you could imagine. Around and around this parade of trucks would cruise the parking lots. Remember I said it was like a big party? It reminded me of growing up in Howell, MI, every night there would be a parade of supped up cars cruising from the Kroger parking lot to the recreation center on the other side of town. Back and forth all night most not knowing what exactly they were looking for, or truth be known wouldn't have a clue as to what to do with it, him or her if they got it anyway. Even when I was a kid with my own 68 GTO I hardly ever stuck around and participated in this nightly American ritual. Anyway there I sit; the parking spot next to me opened up and in comes this shabby, dirty Kenworth cab over. Inside was this driver who looked like he just came out of some holler in Virginia, long hair, beard down to his chin, and in general appeared to be as unkempt as his truck. What was so unusual about this was that there was a much younger girl sitting in the passenger seat. This all seemed somewhat out of place at first glance but considering where I was I didn't give it much thought. I sat there and wondered how in the hell this turd of a driver could entice such a young good looking girl into his truck. But after some deep deliberating thought while smoking my pipe, I figured the old adage holds true that just when you think you've seen it all, something else will come along and prove your simple mind false.

After ten minutes or so she goes back in their bunk and reappears in a bikini. Well now, this could get rather interesting I said to myself. Then she climbs out the window and seductively proceeds to climb onto the roof. She crawls in a very awkward sexy way over to the driver's side, while doing this show she had to climb over the clearance lamps, and the air horns. If she didn't look so hot in her bikini it would have been a bit comical. This unexpected show of exhibitionism in the truck stop parking lot was starting to get interesting indeed. Bending over in a most provocative manner, she reaches down and comes up with a bottle of suntan lotion and a towel and lays it down, has herself a seat and proceeds to slather the oil on herself in the sexiest way she knows how.

I thought by now the CB would be going berzirk, I reached up, turned it on low so it was just barely hearable. Sure enough she had the attention of every driver in there. Looking out my windshield, the trucks doing the parade thing were starting to back up as they all wanted a look at this free show of oiled female flesh. I thought it was sad that these drivers didn't realize that the Pacific Ocean was only 50 miles or so away and there would be a lot better and a lot more babes to google at. But you must realize that a truck stop parking lot is not exactly a hot bed of mental health.

Anyway, sitting there taking all this in, I hear a knock on my passenger door, and this driver and his cohort climb up on my cab and start looking thru my cab at said babe. What the hell do you two want, I ask?

Hey driver we're parked right behind ya, sell us your spot. Now it didn't take a brain surgeon to figure out that with all the attention this girl was getting that things could get a bit crazy in a short time. I was already thinking about moving as I thought this whole charade had the probability of turning out not so good.

What is it worth to you, I asked?

We'll give you 30 bucks man! Come over to the other side, I said.

Over they came, think of Gomer Pyle meets Jethro Clampet meets Barney Fife and add on 140 pounds of belly that sums those two up pretty well. I looked at these two sorry looking bastards and actually felt sorry for them, as they stood there with their tongues hanging out, with a far away starry look in their eyes.

Tell you what, give me 20 and it's all yours, I said. Man that 20 dollar bill flew out the taller ones pocket. Go back to your truck; be ready to pull in when I pull out as it won't take but second for someone to grab this spot. Those two ran back to their truck, jumped in the cab and waved that they were ready. Attempting to pull out I had to wait for the parade to stop so I could move. You should have heard all the chatter on the CB; one would have thought I had just sold the family jewels and the farm. Those drivers thought I was certifiably crazy. (Yup that's me in a nutshell)

For some reason I figured this was not going to turn out well for all concerned. Proceeding around the lot I found another spot a couple rows back. The CB was still a buzz with chatter. You would have thought Hue Heffner had just dropped off a harem of playboy bunnies.

Me, I was thinking more on the lines of a free steak dinner with my new found wealth of twenty dollars. Considering where I was, I figured this was turning out quite nicely for yours truly. After shutting down the truck and locking up, I went into the restaurant in search of nice big, fat steak. Walking into the restaurant I spotted Steve Denny one of our other drivers siting there waving his arm trying to get my attention to come over and sit with him. I knew Steve was in the area but had thought he was supposed to load out that day.

Hey, Dave have a seat, I've been waiting for you man.

How did you know I'd be here? Did dispatch tell you? I didn't see you pull in, how long have you been here?

No one told me you were here, while I was pulling in I heard them talking on the radio that a girl was on top of a truck in a bikini slathering up catching some rays, and that she was parked next to a shiny Freightliner with a surfboard on top of it, and as you're the only person in the world that fits that description wa la, here you are. By the way you're buying diner. How much did you get for that spot?

Laughing I told him it was enough to cover a couple steak dinners. We sat there and devoured steak and caught up on the scuttlebutt of the happenings on the road. We were so into what we were talking about that we hadn't noticed that the restaurant had all but cleared out.

Right about this time we took notice of this, I had a fleeting thought that maybe everyone went out to see the girl on the truck when our waitress came up and asked us why we weren't out watching the strip show in the lot.

Steve and I looked at each other and just about lost it. Well, I said, we had heard about a swim suit with a girl in it. But nothing about a strip show. Things must have progressed in the past hour or so.

Yup, she said, she's up on some truck in a short skirt, high heels and a tube top with the undivided attention of most every driver in both truck stops dancing to a boom box, having a good old time judging from what I've heard.

Do tell, Steve said, sounds like trouble with a capital T, maybe it's best we just stay right here.

I said to the waitress, if we want to see scantily clad women we'd go to the beach. She seemed to like that. Next thing we know she comes over with two huge pieces of apple pie with ice cream and a ton of whipped cream on top.

Here you boy's go, it's on the house, it's refreshing to meet a couple of drivers with some common sense. And it's been a pleasure waiting on you two and not having to listen to lewd comments and being harassed for a date.

We're here in the same boat you are, just doing a job trying to make a living and pay the bills, hoping that we have a little left over for some fun with our friends and family, I said to her. So we sat there and ate our pie talking to her and some of the other waitresses and manager, in general we had a great time. We left a huge tip, and then went to pay the bill, the manager was at the register and said, it's on the house drivers, have a good trip.

Wow, thank you sir, I said, then went over to our booth and laid that twenty on the table. The time spent talking to Steve and the wait staff sure seemed like a better way to spend time, than watching some lame brain twit dance around on top of a truck and watch take her clothes off.

After cruising through the travel store we went out to the lot. Steve was going to the phone stalls at the fuel desk to call his wife, I wanted to stretch out and read a book. I've always been a reader and kicking back smoking my pipe with a good book, was a great way to relax then as it now thirty some years later.

Not being interested in what the latest happening in the lot was, I switched the CB from channel 19 to 12 which was our company channel, just in case Steve or one of our other drivers coming in needed any help. After lighting my pipe I started to read. Not being all that ready for the bunk just yet I reclined the seat back and began to enjoy the rest of the evening. Not long thereafter

Steve gave me a call on the radio, hey Dave things are starting to get out of hand up here.

This didn't surprise me in the least. So what's going down, I asked?

Well I'm parked not too far from where you were before you sold your spot and there are about two dozen cop cars and three or four ambulances. I can't see what exactly is happening but it doesn't look so good. Let's go to 19 and maybe we can find out, he said.

Flipping to channel 19 it didn't take but a short time to get the gist of what all the commotion was about. As it got darker the wilder the goings on became, the dancing bimbo was performing amateur hour on top of the dirty Kenworth. We learned that it was true that the bimbo changed outfits and was indeed doing a bit of strip tease, not to be outdone by an outsider the local ladies of the night (lot lizards) had started to perform on top of the neighboring trucks. Then the party really went into full swing as people showed up with beer, whisky, pot, and whatever they snorted up or shot up. The drivers were shining flashlights up to where the girls performed, then the girl that started it all slipped and fell, when she fell she came down and cracked her head on one of the air horns, broke her arm and ankle or foot. Now picture this for a minute, a hundred or more not so bright truck drivers all messed up on some kind of substance watching this show with god only knows what was going on in their head, watching this show with dozens of flashlights shining, their all a long way from home and they're all thinking, man, it sure don't get any better than this here. Then one of the performers falls and she can't get up. Every one of those idiots, were going to the rescue, all of them probably thinking they are doctors, they are going to save the damsel in distress. Yeah, like that's going to work! A riot occurred, over said self-proclaimed instant medical professionals, which led to the police being called. This was still in the process of going down while Steve and I listened in on the radio.

I signaled to Steve to go back to the company channel, I told him that we were lucky not to be involved in any of that horse shit. I'm hittin the bunk; meet you inside around seven thirty in the AM. After crawling into the bunk I turned on the TV, as it was a little after 11:00 I thought I'd catch the news.

I couldn't believe it the truck stop was on the damn news! They showed the police handcuffing drivers that could hardly stand up, and the lot lizards too. They filmed car after car taking away the unruly and the drunk, more than a few were being loaded into ambulances. On the news it looked like a scene out of a movie, I shook my head, switched off the set, read for a while and went to sleep.

Meeting Steve in the restaurant the next morning we found out what had transpired. Over 40 drivers were arrested for drunk and disorderly conduct, about the same number arrested for drugs, and over 20 people taken away by ambulance. The girl that started it all broke several bones, and another girl fell off the top of another truck and hit the ground when the police showed up. From all the speculation we heard she didn't fair too well either.

After breakfast neither of us had a load till the next day, both of us were to pick up in Long Beach, California the next day. With the whole day to ourselves we decided we'd head over to Long Beach and park at Pier 59 and take a tour of the QUEEN MARY, have lunch on the ship, then catch a whale watching boat ride that evening.

Heading out of the parking lot we seen the aftermath of the night before, what a mess, there were beer and booze bottles strewn around the lot, you could see blood stains where people had been injured, a bunch of trucks had bright orange impound stickers on the windshields. The place looked like a war zone. That's what you get when there's a mob; mentality goes right out the window. (No pun intended) Thinking back I'm thankful to my pipe, in which I could take more enjoyment, than participating in bad entertainment. My pipe is my buddy, always has been, always will be.

Traveling throughout the west I always thought about the pioneers that came before us, who settled this great country. Can you imagine what it would be like to leave from the Midwest in a wagon train with women and children besides all of your belongings and the livestock! There were no roads just a guide, and there was no solid guarantee that he knew exactly where they were going either. Besides a journey like that taking months, what was there waiting for them, once they arrived at wherever it was they were going. More times than not, nothing would be there. They built from the ground up, anything that needed building. That had to be tough, talk about living your dream those people took it to a whole new level in a basically primitive era.

I feel very fortunate to have had the opportunity to see as much of the west as I did, seeing signs that said next services 100 or more miles was a great time to enjoy a few pipe bowels. I never seemed to get tired of the vast amounts of space. Being from the east where you had space but nothing like the west. In the west one can be on top of a mountain or hill and it's common to see for what appears to be 20-30 miles and there are times you actually can.

One trip that had me on the road for a month or more, I unloaded on the Oregon coast and returned to Roseburg for some long awaited R&R. My neighbor had a dog that gave birth to a litter of puppies. Always wanting a dog of my own I picked one out or rather he picked me. These puppies were a mix of Blue Healer/Australian Shepherd this little guy was the coolest looking dog I'd ever seen. From the first time I held him we were a pair. I named him Kenworth, after the first truck I drove over the road, K.W. for short. He had black and white fur with a bunch of silver splotches for a coat. He would be my constant companion for fifteen and a half years. Being a stock dog K.W. loved anything he thought he could heard. Cows were his favorite, though I never had to worry about locking my truck as he thought it was just as much his as it was mine.

There was one time when he was about six or seven months old that comes to mind as I write about him that scared the daylights out of me. I had picked up a load of kiln dried 2 by 4 studs for a subdivision somewhere around the San Francisco Bay area and had arrived at the construction site to unload the night before and thought this is cool, I'll let K.W. out to run a little then kick back, read a book and get a good night's sleep. Then I'd be rested and be able to drive strait back home tomorrow. Even though I had a well laid plan, things that evening didn't work out as well as hoped.

After finding a place to park I let Dubber (short for K.W.) out so he could do important dog things. While I undid my tarps and loosened the straps on the load, I looked around to seen Dubber bounding over a mound of dirt after a few coyotes. Oh shit, I feared my little buddy was a goner. Grabbing the biggest flashlight I had I went off in hot pursuit. I could hear the bunch of them howling, but couldn't get Dubber to come back to me. After about 3 hours I really started to worry. I had never had a child of my own so K.W. was like a kid to me. As barren as this place was and pitch black as it was getting I was more than a little concerned of getting lost myself. So after finding my way back to the truck, I fired it up and turned every light on and waited, still calling his name. After what seemed like forever but in actuality was an hour or so here he comes. His poor ass was dragging, tongue hanging out the side of his mouth, tail wagging and acting proud as could be. I couldn't stay mad at him, just getting him back was good enough for me. He sure was full of himself though.

After unloading in the early A.M, I got dispatched to pick up a load in the heart of the redwoods in northern California. If you've never seen these majestic trees up close its hard to explain just how big they are. That load went to Vail, Colorado to an upscale condo development. So much for going straight home, if I said that I was disappointed I'd be lying as that was part of what I did for a living that always made me look forward to my next run as I never knew where I'd be off to next. Some drivers that I knew only wanted to run from point A to point B turn right around and head home. I, not knowing what I might be transporting or where it had to go was part of the mystique in my feeble mind. Just as long as I had the tools necessary to secure whatever needed loading, with my pipe tobacco and a few cigars, along with a fairly up to date map I was good to go. I was after the adventure of traveling to new places and meeting new people. Besides a love of driving, the people along the way I'd meet were always interesting.

In those days, before the lumber crash of the late 80's, I loaded quite often out of smaller family owned lumber mills. What I enjoyed most when picking up at these mills was going into the offices and seeing the old pictures on the walls of the history of the area I was in. Just gazing at how logging was accomplished in days of yore was awesome indeed. Logging in the modern era seemed easy as machines and diesel engines came into being, and not using steam engines and horses. Also the chainsaw had an enormous effect on being able to fell trees. Looking at some of the old pictures, I would see men standing by a huge Douglas fir that they had felled. After it was felled they still had to limb it then buck (cut it into 20-30 foot length logs) it out so they could load the log onto a train, truck, or run it down a slew into a river where they would raft them up and transport them to a mill or to be loaded onto ships. Now consider that this was all done with whip saws, I'm sure you've seen old time pictures of those long saws with a two fisted handle on each end. Like I mentioned earlier the history of logging never ceased to amaze me.

Smoking a pipe while in some of these older smaller mills, opened more than a few doors for me as I would more times than not meet some mill workers with a pipe in their mouth or one in their pocket. It never ceased to bring a smile to the mill workers I met. I heard horror stories of my fellow drivers going into more than a few of these mills and getting a bad time from the owners or the workers. Hell, come to think of it, as Bob Bitchin has always preached even to this day. It's all about one's attitude, if a person possesses an attitude that is anything but open and positive they will more often than not receive the same in return. This can result in a bad outcome for all concerned. Why there are people trudging through life with such a sour outlook on life has made me feel sorry for them as they just don't get how lucky they are and they have not a clue that life is shining right in front of them and they choose to cast the brightness aside as if it were some fowl smelling ugly entity. Many times I would arrive at my destination and find the folks I had to deal with in a not so chipper mood. The reason for which I had no idea but given a bit of time with them I could usually deciefer what was causing them to be in such a bad mood. If people just took the time to listen to others, bad situations could be turned around to benefit all concerned more times than not. Granted, most folks laboring away in these mills were not generally well educated, but they were working at a hard and dangerous job. Unless a person worked for one of the big lumber mills such as Boise Cascade they were not earning union scale wages. They did the best that they could do for their families by working hard and never turning down overtime or a weekend shift. Work in the lumber industry was hard, dangerous work.

I recall one load in particular when after unloading in Seattle, Washington I got sent to a town named Humptulips, Washington which was 30 or so miles north of Aberdeen, Washington on Route 101. The load was a full truck load of cedar shake shingles going to a development site in southern California. Arriving about ten a.m. I couldn't believe this place, it was small and I do mean small. It was just a pavilion with some shake cutting machines, a rack to buck out the logs into shingle lengths, stacks of pallets, a banding station where they would band bundles of shakes together then put them on a pallet. Once the pallet was full it stood about eight feet high then it was loaded onto trailers. On this morning someone in dispatch had made a mistake and sent me there a day early they only had two pallets ready. This was a typical winter Washington day, cold about 35 degrees, steady rain that keeps coming down with no letup in site for days. The kind of wet cold that chills you to the bone. The workers at this mill must have been getting paid piece work or they had overtime in mind as at first sight of me pulling in they were not too happy, then once they found out the owner/boss wanted to load me that day instead of coming back the next day or having the possibility of me leaving and them not able to get another truck for days, he asked me if I could wait around and load that day. He assured me that I could be loaded in five to six hours. My delivery date in Southern California allowed me some fudge time so I agreed to wait and get the load.

After letting K.W. out to do his thing I caught up on paperwork and was just kind of hanging out watching the way they were making these shakes. One of the workers injured his hand and that slowed the production down so I volunteered to take his place, what he was doing looked like fun, feeding the cedar log blocks into a splitting machine that split the cedar into a perfect shake. While offering my help I pulled a corn cob pipe out of my down vest pocket and started to lite up asking the owner if he minded if I smoked. He got this big grin on his mug and pulled out a battered old pipe of his own. We're gonna get along just fine he told me.

In one corner under the pavilion there was an old Ben Franklin wood stove that was kept full and when the wind blew just right would throw heat our way. K.W. was having a grand time doing dog things all around the mill and checking all the workers out, while doing this he got soaking wet so he laid by the stove to get warm and then have to go recheck everything again. Working with these people of the woods was a treat for me as they had one interesting story after another they told me about all day. The work was cold, hard and a bit risky as you had to move your hands in rhythm with the machines and the other workers or you stood a good chance of losing a finger or hand. That most defiantly could put a damper on one's life.

What should have taken six hours ended up taking nine hours, I didn't mind at all. The mill workers were truly amazed that a truck driver would stick around and wait let alone help them do their job. I laughed and informed them that I was anything but just another truck driver. After taking a late lunch break we went back to it. Finely we finished up and got it loaded. The workers all asked if I needed help to tie the load down but I refused as I knew they were wet and tired and had families to get home to, Roger the owner stuck around for a bit but had to leave as he had a school function to attend with his daughter. He stocked up the stove for me and left the outside light on. Now strapping a load of shakes down is no fast and easy undertaking when it's raining, cold, slippery and not much light. The straps I used were 4 inch lumber straps that were always used in the northwest for lumber as you didn't want to damage the lumber products on your trailer. The pallets were in rows of two all the way down the length of the trailers. They were tall and rickety, as they had a tendency to sway this way and that way. I put what we called V boards on the edge of each stack on both sides, one strap would tighten on one side and the other would tighten on the opposite side, so that you were pulling the load down in two directions to make it more secure, then the lateral straps went on over the cross straps. These went from the bottom of the front of the trailer to bottom rear where they would secure onto rollers and get as tight as you could get them. Now picture crawling around on top of this load on wet cedar putting V boards on, making sure every strap was positioned just right with a flashlight dark as sin and trying not to fall off, after all your up 13 feet 6 inches and a fall from that height is gonna more than hurt and with nobody around but K.W. it was quite the process.

After spending an hour and a half securing everything and putting my extra equipment away K.W. and I went under the pavilion next to the stove to warm up and dry out the best we could. Sitting there by the stove with my dog next to me a pipe in my mouth dead assed tired, I thought a normal person would be miserable, pissed off or at the very least have a bad attitude. Not me, I sat there looking around at the stacks of huge cedar logs my fully loaded truck with all the lights burning and gazing around at the tall fir and cedar trees. My thought was how fortunate I was to be there at that time and place.

After we dried out and warmed up we were on the road again. By this time it was going on eleven p.m., we trucked out of Washington into Oregon about 100 miles south of Portland to a 76 Truck Stop near Corvallis, OR, I hung up all my wet clothes in the front of the cab, fed K.W. and myself, lit my pipe grabbed a book, kicked back in the bunk and thought what cool day. Being able to do what I had done, the people I met, and the opportunity to work in the mill, even though it rained all day and night I didn't care, as long as my truck ran, K.W. was with me and I had a pipe to smoke I was happy.

Speaking of my west coast famous dog K.W., another run comes to mind as I sit here writing this. There were seven or eight of us that picked up loads out of Sun Studs in Roseburg, Oregon going to a job site in Las Vegas, Nevada. After unloading there we went outside of Vegas to a gypsum plant and loaded sheet rock for some new subdivision around Los Angeles. We agreed to meet at Whisky Pete's on our way to Los Angeles we had some time to spare so a few guys went down the strip since back then you could do that with a truck. This was before the strip morphed into what it would later become. Drivers could usually park behind a casino if not on the strip itself. I went to the 76 Truck Stop west of town, fueled then preceded to Pete's. A little history about Pete is in order before I get any further with what took place that night.

For about 10 months before this night Whisky Pete's was undergoing a major rebuild on the north side of the I-15 at Exit 1 in Nevada, it was the first exit after dropping off the mountain in California. Before this major transformation of the acreage of what used to be Whisky Pete's it was not much more than a few cobbled together houses of questionable construction, harboring inside a bar, restaurant and the gaming slots and tables. The place smelled like 50 year old cigarette smoke and stale beer. Across the freeway there was a joint called Jane's Place much smaller and more dilapidated than Pete's.

Pulling into the parking lot that evening we had seen that the new improved Whisky Pete's was open for business. This place was huge, I must say that it was impressive, the parking lot was enormous. Right in the middle after pulling in they had this corral made of this decorative split rail fence with 40 to 50 head of cattle in it.

Red Stevens, Steve Denny and I parked next to Don and Nolan two of the other drivers we were to meet up with. I let K.W. out to do his thing and to run a bit, then while talking to Steve and Red I lit up my pipe while walking around the truck checking my load. K.W. never strayed too far from me or the truck so I was surprised that he wasn't to be seen. The three of us started calling for him and here he comes, tail up waging like crazy, this big grin on his mug with his tongue hangin out the side of his snout. I said Dubber what have you been up to? Then this cow comes running by right in front of us. Just barley did I get my hand on his caller or he would have been gone. Just then we started hearing truck air horns and car horns going off all around us. The three of us looked at each other then at K.W. oh shit Dubber what did you do? We were standing by the driver's door of my truck and could hear people on the C.B. screaming about cows all over the freeway and parking lot. Well, Steve and Red knew K.W. was just as crazy if not worse than his owner, quick get him in the truck, I put Dubber in the cab, Red suggested we split like right now. No I said, earlier I promised K.W. a hamburger for diner; let's get inside, check out the new place, besides Don and Nolan are probably 2 beers up on us by now. If we leave we might look guilty. What the hell do you mean WE, he's your crazy assed dog, Red said to me.

Oh hell no, Steve says, he's our crazy assed company mascot we need to get inside, act normal and let things cool down out here besides everyone agreed to spend the night here, hurry up we need to get inside.

So we start heading for the door, as we approach we see a bunch of people trying to corner a cow that looked like it wanted to trample someone. Once inside we located Don and Nolan in the restaurant, sitting at a big table with two pitchers of beer and a stack of Whisky Pete's official libation glasses. We took a seat and told them what just happened. Now if you haven't figured it out yet, K.W. went right into the corral and herded those cattle right thru that cheesy split rail fence. We sat there laughing our ass off. About 40 minutes later the rest of the gang arrived, said it was like bedlam out there with cows everywhere.

After explaining what just transpired we all gave a toast to K.W. we were all quite proud of him. I started to order K.W. a hamburger but Don said he deserved a steak, seeing as how he did such a good job of doing what a stock dog was born to do.

Taking the box with K.W.'s sirloin out to him I saw police blooper lights everywhere. It looked like everybody and there brother thought they were cowboys and were trying the best they could to round up the critters. After watching K.W. enjoy his steak for a minute I went back inside and told the guy's to grab an extra pitcher and come outside and enjoy the show. So that's exactly what we did for the next hour or so. A couple of the drivers in our group were real cowboys so they got a bigger kick from watching this wild parking lot cattle drive.

Back inside we all had a steak dinner then indulged in more than a few more beers. Don and I enjoyed our pipe's while the others smoked there smoke of choice. All in all it was a very entertaining evening. I gave my buddy extra treats that night. (I never said he was a TRAINED stock dog.)

About 2 weeks later I stopped there again, no more cows, no more split rail fence. Huh, wonder what changed their minds. Giving K.W. a scratch behind his ear I said, good boy Dubber, we can always use more parking spaces.

Another area I enjoyed driving thru was the Red Woods in Northern California and Southern Oregon. Hell, as long as I was on the coast I was happy. The Route 101 and the P.C.H. (Pacific Coast Highway) were always a pleasure to drive. There seemed to be something magical about driving thru those gigantic trees, especially at night. There used to be this old café in the heart of the red woods that stayed open late for the truckers and had ample parking. Outside just before you walked in the door was a hollowed out red wood that you could walk thru. Inside there was a real nickelodeon and it still worked.

Trucking thru that area I had a few favorite roadside picnic areas that I would stop and spend the night right next to the Pacific Ocean, with the ocean breeze flowing thru the cab, enjoying my pipe and looking at the moon shine off the water was truly a sight to behold. I was able to experience that quite a few times. Anytime that I had a bad day or was someplace that was less than desirable I would think about my special chosen places, which seemed to outweigh the bad.

CHAPTER IV

LOGGING

After a few years of running all over the west I wanted to try my hand at log trucking as things on the road were getting a little too boring for me. I wanted to get up into the mountains more than I could just trucking over the same mountain passes all the time.

As with oil field work, logging is hard, dirty, and dangerous work. That being said it's also fun if you possess the right attitude. Logging in the Pacific Northwest is different than in other parts of the country, the trees and the terrain make the difference. I don't know what it's like now, but back then you had to know somebody or be related to someone to get into logging, luckily I had built a good reputation on the road and the truck I drove was popular as it had won the Douglas County Timber Days Festival Truck Show and a few others truck shows around the west. So getting my foot in the door was difficult, but not impossible. Wanting to do this type of work with a passion made a difference too.

After talking it over with a few friends that were into logging, I thought it would be a blast to work in the woods as a logger than get back into a truck. Through a friend of a friend I met Ken Wahl, he was a tree faller. After a side of timber was purchased he would go in and fell the trees, limb them, and cut (buck) them into lengths to be hauled (yarded) up the side of the mountain then loaded onto trucks headed for a lumber mill, where they got processed into whatever was to be done with them such as plywood, lumber, beams, or whatever.

It took me a while but I talked Ken into teaching me how to do this type of work. Him being a pipe and cigar man himself, we got along pretty well. I thought it would be cool as anything I had ever done to go up into the mountains and cut down big ass fir trees.

Let me tell you that was fun. Getting up real early at 3:00 a.m. and depending where you were falling that day, being on the mountain, checking your gear before the sun came up. Ken liked to use either Stihl or Huskavarna saws. He had several of each. I got a good deal on a big Stihl chain saw that would handle up to or over a four foot bar. This saw was a beast, slim and light compared to the older saws used just four to six years before I came along. Ken had been falling timber for 20 plus years and he still had all his limbs, fingers and toes. He'd been hurt a few times but nothing too serious. Besides him being 27 years older than myself he had a shit load of experience in the mountain forests. Tall, lanky, sort of quiet, with a big walrus mustache, Ken looked natural with a bent poker pipe in his mouth. Neither of us would smoke a cigar in the mountains as there was too good of a chance the ash could fall off prematurely, possibly starting a fire.

Working high up in the mountains I got to see things that normal people only get to see on National Geographic if at all. It's hard to explain the feeling you get when your cutting an old growth tree that stands about 200 feet tall. To this day people have the misguided opinion that these types of trees shouldn't be logged. Just so you understand, let me explain to you that the phrase, log it or lose it holds true. Old growth timber is very dry and the terrain below them is like tinder. All the forest fires in the spring, summer and fall are more times than not started by lightning strikes, misuse of campfires or a careless actions by humans. If the old growth timber is logged and the area is reforested it becomes greener therefore not as likely to burn so easily. It really pisses me off to see these environmentalist do gooders that have no concept of what is happening in the real world that want to preserve every tree, bush and blade of grass. Then without fail we watch old growth timber go up in flames, polluting our environment with all the smoke. Besides, new growth creates more oxygen; don't these wacko do gooders enjoy breathing better air? Seems to me that they would rather see good timber go to waste and bitch about us smoking a cigar or pipe. Where's the logic in that I ask you, anyway enough of that on with the adventure.

Going up into the mountain forests you had to dress for the occasion as regular clothing would and could get you killed or maimed in such a way as to ruin the rest of your life. If you've ever watched axe men filmed in the Pacific Northwest you notice that everyone in the woods does not have seams on the bottom of their pants and there loose fitting, held up by suspenders. The reason behind this is that if a log gets loose and you have run away from it your pant seems could catch on a snag or something and hold you back, stumble, or fall, resulting in getting your ass crushed by a log. Besides that you wore a bright colored hardhat and a safety vest so the crew up on the landing or fellow chocker setters on the site could see you. The boots were special also, called logging boots, depending on the preference of the logger they went from 6 inches to just below your knee most guys would opt for cork boots that had sharp spikes on the bottom similar to a golf shoe. Losing your footing walking on a log or whatever could mess you up indeed.

You could always spot a tree faller by the gear hanging off them, such as a special large round tape masseur clipped to their belt and a cushioned pad on their shoulder to balance the huge chainsaw they carried up and down the mountains, besides that we would have an assortment of wedges to hammer into the tree with an axe to help persuade the tree to fall in the desired direction, these came in a variety of lengths and thicknesses. Plus you had to carry your gas and oil for the bar on the saw and a few good files to keep the chain supper sharp as a dull chain was dangerous and a waste of time. And don't forget your lunch, coffee, and water to drink. For Ken and myself we always had our pipe and tobacco with us.

Being in my late 20's I was still full of energy, so climbing up and down the mountains was no big deal. Ken would swing by my place, pick me up, and go to the café for coffee then up the mountain we'd go. Felling those big trees was a real challenge at times we had to fell them in such a way so they could be yarded up the side of the mountain the easiest way. Some landings were set up to do high lead logging while others for just plain yarding the logs up, and some were even done by hot air balloon, while in extreme cases they even used those big assed sky crane helicopters.

We always smoked a pipe bowl on the way up the mountains, at lunch break, and then on our way home. Listening to Ken tell of logging in years past was a treat as the stories were interesting and full of crazy characters. Speaking of which, I met my share of crazy people while I was in the logging industry. All of which I would not want to be on the wrong side of. They were all good natured as a whole, just don't piss them off.

One job in particular always comes to mind when I think back on those days. We were cutting on a mountain side on the coast by Newport, Oregon, North of Coos Bay, Oregon. This side had a high ridge where the landing was going to be. That's where they yard up the logs and load them onto trucks then brand the log so when the driver gets to the mill to unload they know where and who the log came from. Branding was done with an axe style tool that had a big stamp like brand which was smacked into the butt of the log, taking a log off a landing without a brand was illegal.

The side we were felling timber on was quite high and faced the ocean. Starting at the bottom we cut our way up the side to the ridge. The loggers wanted the option of using a few tall trees on top of the ridge to yard timber up the slope. Ken picked out a few choice trees on top and on the last day we worked that site we brought along our climbing gear. That type of equipment is called spurs in the woods which consists of strapping on these spike type spurs to the inside of your boots and calves, then there is a strong thick leather belt that you wear with shackles on each side to attach a climbing rope to so you can scale up the tree and top it. This sort of cutting is a blast, climbing up anywhere from 50 to 100 feet up you can get a great view of your surrounding area. The day before on our way home Ken told me to pack a good lunch the next day as we would eat lunch up in the tree after we cut the tops off.

That morning I packed a pair of binoculars in with my pipe and lunch. We arrived at the work site, cut a few, then up on the ridge put on our climbing gear, attached lines to our saws and lunch then scaled the trees. What a trip that was. Climbing up about 50 feet we positioned ourselves, pulled up our saws and chose a direction we wanted the tops to fall and started cutting. When you're up that high and you top a tree such as we were doing, when the top of the tree falls the bottom has a tendency to sway back and forth like a bucking bronco, this was fun, and I was getting paid for this! After toping and riding the bronco tree, we sat up on the stumps, hauled our lunches up and enjoyed the view. This was totally tits man. Looking to the west we could see the ocean, what a site, I could see big ships for the lumber industry heading in and out of Newport. Sitting up there looking out over all the timber we had cut and seeing the Pacific Ocean, smoking my pipe after eating was something you never forget, I felt truly blessed to be fortunate enough to be there.

I worked another few months with Ken then decided to get back into a truck hauling logs looked like fun. Finding a company in Winston, Oregon who had around 40 trucks I started log trucking. Thinking back maybe the fact that I didn't have a whole lot of time to smoke might have swayed me into a truck again, truth be told I just plain dig driving, it doesn't really matter what as long as I'm behind the wheel I'm happy. Usually I would smoke my pipe going for my first load of the day and on the way to the mill on the last load that day. The time in between I smoked cigars or cigarettes. Having a well-stocked tobacconist in town came in handy as I could at times after unloading at certain mills in Roseburg swing by park my truck close to if not right across the street and pop in and grab whatever I needed.

Driving a log truck in the northwest was way cool and a bunch of fun. Hell, I thought I was a damn good driver until I started doing that. It was very different from anything I had driven. Most of the trucks where I worked had a ten speed main transmission and a four speed axillary transmission. So there were many choices of gear combinations to choose from depending on what type of grade and terrain you were navigating over. The logging roads were only wide enough for one truck at a time with dozens of pull off spots going up and down the mountains, a driver coming down the mountain with a load on had the right of way as it's not easy to stop a loaded truck on the grades we were on. Therefore you had to talk your way up and down with the CB radio as each mountain side had a specific channel assigned to it. You were basically driving blind, what with all the switchbacks, trees, and what not visibility was limited. That being said, you were too busy trying not to get run over or drive off the side of the mountain, to take the time to smoke a pipe, but a cigar was just the ticket as it was easier to clamp in your mouth.

I've always enjoyed the taste of a good cigar, or what I thought was good at that time. Through the years I've met more than a few people that wouldn't smoke a cigar but just chew on them or in the case of my good friend David Vesconi basically ate them, each to his own, right! More on David Vesconi later, this guy is one of the most colorful characters you will ever read about. Myself I never acquired the knack or the taste for chewing or eating a cigar.

One day in particular comes to mind about chewing cigars. It was in the middle of winter and we were hauling logs off one of the bigger mountains east of Roseburg. The landing we were on was up high, about 9 thousand feet, it had been snowing hard all day something like a foot per hour and this white shit was getting damn deep in a hurry. I'd better explain that in order to operate in these conditions you had to put chains on your tires or you weren't going anywhere, we called it hanging iron, as that sums it up as these chains were big and heavy, done the right way it didn't take long to chain up the truck and trailer. That day I was first up which meant I was the first truck on the landing that morning. On my way up for my first trip as soon as I pulled off the main road I chained up, and up the hill I went easy as could be, while on the landing it took more time than usual to get loaded as the choker setters down the side that hooked up the logs to be yarded up to the landing were having a tough time of it as the snow was really coming down making their job very difficult indeed. While waiting to get my load on another truck showed up, then an hour after that another truck arrived, it was starting to get crowded up there, after what seemed like forever I was loaded and bailed off the mountain with the snow coming down in those big huge flakes that look so picturesque . While dropping off the mountain I figured the snow would stop the closer to sea level I got, not so that day as it came down all the way to the mill.

After unloading at Sun Studs in Roseburg off I went to grab another load, I got on the company two-way Radio and informed the log boss on that site I was on my way back up. After getting the go ahead to come back up, I was off again. As much as the conditions permitted I hauled ass back, then I got a call on the 2 way from the landing wanting to know where I was. By then I was close to three quarters of the way back, they thought I would be farther out than what I was. They said things weren't going very well and that the 2 other trucks were still up there. Being as close as I was turning around wasn't gonna make the company any money. After deliberating for a few minutes they said to keep on strolling their way. Not more than 5 minutes after that I was still on the main road and I had to pull over and chain up my drive tires or I wasn't going anywhere. Things started to go from bad to worse in a hurry. Don't get me wrong, I lived for this kind of shit, the worse it got the better I liked it. Adverse conditions really tripped my trigger, when all your senses are on high alert knowing that just one wrong move, miscalculation, or decision and your ass was history was addicting to me. I turned onto the road leading up to the landing, got on the CB and said I was at the 1 mile stick and headed up empty, a driver from another company answered back saying he was at the 2 coming down sliding a bit on the switchbacks. No problem I said, after another half mile I used a pull off and waited for him to slide on by.

What the Sam hell are you going back up for? Don't you realize how bad it is up on top? Well judging by what's happening down here I've got a damn good idea I told him. Well good luck to ya.

Your just plain crazy he said. Yeah I'm well aware of this fact I told him. After that it was another 32 miles of logging road up to the landing and I didn't see another truck or pick up the rest of the way. Finally arriving on site things were going pretty slow, one truck was just about loaded so I figured a wait of about 1 to 2 hours and I'd be headed back down to the mill then home. So much for thinking, it took another hour to load the truck that was being loaded and another two and a half hours to get the waiting truck done then it was my turn finally. During this time there was a D-8 Caterpillar bulldozer keeping the landing cleaned of the quickly accumulating snow. That white shit was getting deep in a hurry faster than before. When the first truck was loaded and the driver had secured the load they tied the D-8 to the rear of his trailer so that on the way down if the driver started to lose it or started to go too fast the operator could just drop the blade and that would bring both of them to a halt then they could proceed again. After the first truck the dozer came back and did the same thing to the second truck. While this was happening I thought, well shit man this might be too bad bailing off this hill in all the snow with a bit of an anchor if things get too weird or out of control. After another 2 hours I was loaded, I put 2 wrapper cable chains around the load then pulled forward a ways, got out and put two more on. By this time it was the end of the day, I wasn't paying attention to the crew at all. I just assumed they would wait for me, walking around the rig checking my tire chains something hit me that it was damn quiet around me, looking about I didn't see anyone, no log crew, no chocker setters, or operators. The dozer was sitting there gathering snow and no operator. Shit, this is not good, you know how sometimes you expect to see people around you and then you look about and you just know you're alone and that empty feeling comes over you. That's just what I felt like up on that mountain. The rule is that nobody is left on the mountain alone. I jumped into the cab, got on the 2-way radio and called for the crew asking where the hell everyone went to. We all left they tell me, what about that dozer operator where is he, it's worse now than when the other 2 trucks went down. You're on your own driver let us know if you get in trouble. Well isn't this a royal bitch I'm thinking. Then my boss comes on the radio and asks if I'm going to be able to make it down ok. Sure I said no sweat. I could tell that Rick was as pissed off as I was being left up there alone. Getting out and looking around the snow seemed to be 3 to 4 feet deep I had all my drive tires chained up and the trailer was chained also, what I was concerned with was the steering tires, looking in my chain box I found an old set of single chains that looked as if they hadn't been used in a few years. Giving them a close inspection they looked bad but useable. After putting those on the steer tires I was ready to bail off the mountain, always being up for a challenge this to me was going to be great fun. Any normal person would not be thinking along those same lines but like I mentioned before, I am not normal by any stretch of the word.

Having chained up the steer tires and back in the cab I was ready to bail off the mountain and not being in a hurry I thought a cigar was called for. After sparking up a big fat one I had been saving I was ready. Off I went, the snow was so deep the front bumper was pushing it and some of it was starting to come over the hood and when I would come around a switchback curve it slid off and started gathering again. This worked in my favor as all this snow was helping to hold me back so the rig wasn't gaining too much speed. Things went nice and smooth for a while and I was looking around at all the beautiful sites the snow was making of the area, enjoying my cigar with the driver's side window open so I could hear any strange sounds coming from the rig that might cause me concern or worse. I came around one sharp curve then hit more of a down grade, I touched the brakes a bit to slow down more as up ahead coming up quick was another tight switchback turn. I heard one of those sounds that told me something wasn't right, looking in my mirror I seen that the trailer brakes had locked up and was starting to come around and say hi to me at my window if I didn't do something proper like right now I'd be in deep shit. I let off the brakes and grabbed another gear to gain some speed and stay ahead of the trailer, all of a sudden the next turn was right there and things were getting intense in a big hurry, right then I hit a big bump and chomped down on my cigar, it fell somewhere and I continued to wrestle the truck around said curve, I'm gaining more speed than what is safe so getting around the curve and having the rig all going in the right direction I figured things were going to be just fine. All of a sudden the radio comes on and Rick asks me how I'm doing. Just then I realized I had a mouthful of cigar butt in my mouth, turning my head to the left I spit it out the window as eating it wouldn't taste so good to me, splat the whole dark brown mess went all over my mirror I could still see a little out the thing so that could wait, grabbing the mike I inform him everything is hunky dory. We talked for a bit more then while hanging up the mike my crotch felt like it was on fire, looking down sure enough my crotch was smoking away, the cigar that I thought was on the floor was in my lap instead, shit fire this sucks, raising up I brushed it on to the floor and while doing so burnt the hell out of the back of my hand grabbing some snow from outside the truck I piled it onto my lap to put the embers out. I was still trying my best to keep the truck under control dropping off the mountain; to say I was a little busy would be an understatement. After 25 miles or so things started to calm down and I pulled over and took all the tire chains off and proceeded to the mill. I was glad it was Friday, what a day, I had a ball, even with all that went wrong the truck and I were still in one piece, what more can you ask for? From that day on whenever I see someone chewing on or basically eating a cigar I think back on that day and chuckle to myself.

I really enjoyed hauling logs and seeing all that big country, going up the mountain log roads just before daylight I would often see bears, elk, mountain lions, eagles, owls, goats and more. Arriving first on the landing enjoying a cup of coffee and a pipe watching the sun come up, listening to the critters was quite a remarkable way to start the day.

Not long after that happened, the tree hugger people started to scream about the spotted owl being run out of the woods because of the logging industry. Even though it had been proven that the little guy could adapt just fine anywhere it wanted to, the tree huggers were starting to gain momentum in their quest to shut down the logging industry. I could see the writing on the wall, when it was all said and done those little Volvo Subaru driving liberal freaky people would sure as shit get their whiny way. Don't they always, the same bunch are the ones whining about pipe smoke, cigarette smoke, or any kind of smoke. The same bunch don't have a word to say when the forest fires burn out of control every year due to all the dry old growth timber, when you see the national news showing clips of the fires and there are acres of smoke in the air. These self-righteous opinionated little do-gooder people are scary. It's best to avoid beings such as they are. Seems like all they want to do is stick their nose in anywhere but in their own backyard. Beware these obnoxious pricks are everywhere.

I'll get back to these entities later on as they do play into my adventures in more ways than I care to dwell on too heavily. Anyway, the tree freaks were gaining more ground every day, knowing how all powerful this group was I knew it wouldn't be long before they had a drastic effect on the logging in that section of the country. Then life happened and I found myself moving to upstate New York on Lake George. Wow what a culture shock that was. Coming from the forests in Oregon then uprooting to New York was a real shock. During the week I hauled yogurt out of a dairy in Saratoga Springs, New York to cold food storage warehouses on the east coast from Portland, Maine to Baltimore, Maryland. Seemed like everywhere I went out there people were just plain pissed off at everything and everybody. There were a few warehouses that I got into that some of the dock workers chewed tobacco a cigar or had an unlit pipe in their mouth. These guys were a lot easier to get along with than the non-tobacco users.

CHAPTER V

EAST COAST

I'm basically pretty much laid back in my attitude. The people I met on the east coast were just to wound up for me. I couldn't wait to get out of there. I did meet some interesting folks out that way. While I traveled about I would stumble upon a tobacconist shop every now and then. One morning I got lost looking for this small cold warehouse in Manhattan. I was traveling down Broadway dodging taxis and the hundreds of little delivery trucks unloading their wares alongside of the street. I don't remember the cross street I was at but off to my left I spotted a cool looking old time Pipe and Cigar shop. Now you must remember that I'm in a 75 foot long 18 wheeler. I really wanted to go into that shop and have a look around. Having just about passed it I assessed the situation, went around the block, pulled in front of the shop, blocking a bunch of cars put my 4 ways on and went into the shop. My rational being that if these thousands of other motorist could inconvenience me with every move I tried to make it was my turn, besides I wasn't planning on being in there too long. Walking in, I felt as if I were stepping back in time. The sign out front was weathered but I did make out it had been there since 1934. The place smelled like many years of fine tobacco, what an enjoyable smell that is. The old timer behind the counter looked at me then out at my rig. Checking out the shop as best I could in the hurry I was in he says, this is a first, in all the 40 years I've been here. Never had anyone block off half the street just to come in here.

Granted it was a bit of a gutsy move but in my feeble mind I was upon a quest to explore an old time pipe shop and that took precedence over the many blaring horns to be heard outside the shop doors.

So what's your pleasure he says.

How about a nice strong cigar around so big I said holding my hands apart 8 to 10 inches. We walked into the humidor and he grabbed a nice looking dark cigar off one of the top shelves. Great I said and took 2 of them. At the counter while he was ringing me up I plucked the top off a tobacco jar to take a whiff. Here he says, that's one of my best sellers. With a big handful he put some in a plastic bag he said here enjoy. Now get outa here before you push some bastard over the edge parked as you are. Thanks I said and took off.

That place was very old and well-worn you could feel the history of the shop standing inside. That is a feeling I would look for in the future. Sometimes I could feel it and other times I wouldn't. But when found you felt comfortable. Kind of like a home away from home.

After a year in New York I had enough, it was time to move back to Michigan. It wasn't that I didn't like New York I did, but Michigan and the Great Lakes were home for me.

CHAPTER VI

BACK IN THE MITTEN

They say that you can never move back to your hometown. This was true in some ways but in others not so much. Upon arriving back in Howell I was fortunate enough to find a small place on Thompson Lake, better known locally as Howell Lake. Growing up in Howell this lake was a major part of my life. My grandparents lived across the street from the lake and across the water from there the public beach. This lake was always special to me as I belonged to the Sea Scouts in my preteen and teen years. It seemed like we were on the lake sailing any chance we got. During the winter we sailed ice boats. These were T shaped made out of wood with a fair sized sail. When conditions were right you could really haul ass with them.

Having been a sailor from way back, when a guy I worked with offered to sell me a 14 foot Cyclone Sailboat for a hundred bucks I jumped at it. With a little work and some spit and polish I was back on the water again. Thinking back on that time I must have been making up for lost time, if there wasn't ice on the water I was sailing.

Being in Howell again was nice as the pace seemed a lot slower than New York but more up to date than Oregon. This was the beginning of the 90s, when the cigar boom took off.

My dad lived in town about 5 miles from the lake. He was a pipe smoker, dad liked pipes that were sturdy good smokers, and Borkum Riff was his tobacco of choice. On birthdays and Christmas I would give him other types of tobacco but he always without fail went back to his trusty standby.

Howell Lake is without a doubt one of the nicest lakes I've ever been on, at around 100 acres it has 3 islands, and 4 separate sections, two of which are divided by a peninsula that stretches out a good ways from land. I lived on the east side of this peninsula on Lakeside Drive about a third of a mile down the same street as my grandmother. At this time I worked for one of the major soft drink manufacturers and worked Monday thru Friday, that left me with the weekends at home. Depending on what shift I was on this left me time to sail even during the week. For a while there I had gotten away from smoking a pipe or cigars. This all changed one day when I sailed around and put in on the big island after spotting an old wooden sailboat tied up to the larger of the two islands in the center of the lake.

The boat I was drooling over was a 1947 Lightning Class Sailboat. This boat was cool as it had that old nautical look to it that the newer fiberglass boats just didn't have, mine included. The lightning was 19 feet 10 inches long, my little hotrod sailboat was only 14 feet.

While I checked this boat out over walked the owner, I immediately recognized the owner as I had worked for him and his wife helping them to move from a house around the corner from where I lived in town to a place they were building in the country about ten miles out. The guy's name was Jim Stuhrberg, he looked like an old sea captain straight out of central casting. Picture Edward Herman with a sea captains beard with white and gray coloring. Jim was smoking a huge cigar, the last time I had seen him 21 years earlier he was into smoking those small Parodi cigars. When I was on the west coast I too smoked them as they are a damn good smoke, those and Avanti cigars I'm sure you know the ones I'm talking about, soaked in Anisette they still remain one of my favorite smokes to this day.

After reacquainting, Jim and I started to meet out on the lake a few times a week and sail. Always smoking a cigar. If Jim wasn't smoking a cigar he always without fail would be puffing on a pipe. He kept a box of Marsh Wheeling cigars in the stern of his boat. The Lightning he and his wife had, had a red hull with a cedar strip around it for a rub rail, a heavy painted canvas deck, the combing, mast and boom were also natural cedar as were the seats and floorboards, with many coats of spar varnish. The inside of the hull was painted white. All in all it was a really good looking boat. From the first time I laid eyes on the boat I wanted one just like it with that special nautical look to it. There's just something about the wood that makes wooden boats so magical.

After getting to know Jim, I started to smoke cigars with more passion than I did in the past. About then I noticed all of Jim's pipes were unique in some way. I wanted a pipe of my own with more personality than the normal shapes available at the not so great smoke shops that I seemed to visit. It had been quite a while since I'd been in a real shop. So one fall day we went to Edwards Tobacco in downtown Ann Arbor. We parked in a parking lot a couple blocks away and walked into this cool tree covered shopping area. It was a bit like walking into Didagean Ally in the Harry Potter movies.

Edwards Tobacconist was in the middle on the right, it wasn't all that big of a shop but then again it didn't have to be. Anything tobacco you could want was well laid out in this small shop, they had pipes, cigars, dozens upon dozens of house mixed blends in jars, besides that a big variety of tinned tobacco seemed to be tucked in wherever they could find space. Jim had told me to keep looking between the cracks if I didn't see much in the display cases. They had pipes of every sort but nothing actually jumped to my attention. We started looking in every nook and cranny in the shop. It wasn't long before Jim found a pipe in the back of a shelf. It was shaped like an acorn, it wasn't briar but some sort of pressed African meerschaum, it wasn't pure white, but more of a light yellow color. The pattern on it looked like a cross between a sandblast and some type of dremel tool with a burr bit sculpted it. This pipe had character to it, I'd never smoked a pipe that smoked so cool and you could really taste the tobacco flavor.

That's all it took for me to start collecting better grade pipes and trying all different types of tobacco. At that time I drove for a company out of Rochester Hills and Livonia, Michigan. I picked up and delivered service parts for GM cars and trucks in Michigan and the surrounding states. This gave me the opportunity to drop in on tobacco shops in a lot of different areas. This was also the time that the cigar craze of the 90's took off. Tobacco shops seemed to pop up everywhere. These new cutting edge shops were basically stick stores where you purchased one, two or more cigars at a time. At first when I started to visit these shops most would not carry pipe tobacco at all. Then more and more of these places started carrying pipe tobacco arranged on the counter in jars or in a corner like a red headed step child. Upon further investigation of these establishments I found that a large percentage of the them carried Lane Pipe Tobacco. Lane makes and blends some very fine tobacco, especially in the bulk blends that were displayed in large glass jars. Besides bulk, some shops would also carry the typical drugstore pouch brands. If you were looking for that feeling you get when you walked into an older smoke shop specializing all things tobacco you were just shit out of luck as this new wave of smoke shop was severely lacking in all categories. These places were extremely new smelling as if to say we're not gonna be here long. Deep down I felt this was going to be a fast flash in the pan. Not to mention the aliens that worked there, they knew absolutely nothing about cigars and even less to do with pipes. Then all the prices on cigars started creeping up what Jim and I once paid $2.50 to $3.25 were selling for more than $5.00. Most all the new fad shops carried pipes and tobacco by the second year of the cigar boom. They were not much more than a glorified display of what you would have found in most drug stores ten or so years ago.

I had a great time looking for tobacco/cigar shops or any type of place that carried cigars and pipe related products besides bulk or pouch tobacco. Knowing I'd be working in a city for a week or more I would scope out how to get to all the tobacconist shops, I could get away with parking my 18 wheeler close enough to walk to quickly, get in and scope the place out to determine if there was anything they had that interested me in pipes, cigars and all the tools one needs to partake in the enjoyment of tobacco whatever your preference may be. Every time I went into a tobacco shop I would always without fail buy something. I had read an article in Pipe Friendly Magazine telling the readership that you must respect and appreciate your local tobacco shop or whatever other shops one might enter and to always buy something as if to say thanks for being there for my tobacco pleasures.

Right around this time Jims wife Lillian past on due to cancer, I had inherited Jim & Lillian's lighting sailboat with the stipulation that I would restore it and would never change the name of Lilun on the stern. While I was in the process of rebuilding the boat Jim would stop by and check out how I was coming along with whatever project I had in the works. Without fail the conversation entailed in depth contemplation about hot rods, sailboats, and tobacco. Jim and I started to go on tobacco runs once a month sometimes two to three times a month depending upon what time of year it was.

During a typical tobacco run we would start off by taking the back roads to downtown Flint, Michigan where Paul's Pipe Shop was located. Walking into Paul's really was like a time warp; Paul had been in the pipe trade for 63 years when I met him in the early 90's. I'm pretty sure he's been in business well over 75 years now. Paul himself doesn't come into the shop much anymore as he is 100 years old now. The day to day running of the shop is done by his son Danny Spanolio who also has a hand in overseeing the goings on of the Arrowhead Pipe Club which is sponsored by Paul's Pipe shop.

Walking into Paul's you are first stunned by the sheer volume of pipes on display in cases lining the walls. Every nook and cranny has something tobacco related stuck in it. I'm not just talking about the display cases; there are pipes all the way to the ceiling. Every type of pipe you could ever imagine can be found if by some type of fluke the certain pipe you are looking for can't be found just tell Danny or another shop clerk what exactly you've got in mind and sure enough they will magically produce what you want from a corner out of sight or in a bottom drawer behind the pipe cases lining the shop. Along the walls beyond the main store sits the pipe hospital where pipes are brought back to life while others just need a minor repair. The walls in this area are covered with memorabilia and pictures of Paul with various celebrities throughout his 80 plus years as a Tobacconist blessed with the old time traditions of the ways of the pipe. Upstairs you'll find a Pipe Museum, one wall of the museum is dedicated to the International Association of Pipe Smokers Clubs better known as I.A.P.S.C. Paul started the I. A.P.S.C. many years ago, and along with it started a pipe smoking contest that is held yearly by the hosting club of that year. Every winner from the first contest to the present has his or her picture along with the winner's pipe, that they used to win and a record of their time. Paul won the contest 6 or 7 times a feat he's quite proud of. I've gone to a number of these pipe show contests followed by an evening dinner. Paul's shop also serves as sponsor for the Arrowhead Pipe club.

One of the things I like most about Paul's is the fact that the store is predominantly about pipes and all things pipe. There is a walk in humidor for cigars and some of the shops choice pipe tobacco. Paul's is so dedicated to everything pipe that the cigar humidor seems a bit out of place. The shop is located in downtown Flint, Michigan that being said it's still worth the trip off the beaten path, most of downtown Flint isn't there anymore but Paul's Pipe Shop still remains in the ruins of a diminishing once vibrant city. I remember going with my parents to visit relatives in Flint and the surrounding suburbs such as Fenton and Grand Blanc. I can still recall what Downtown Flint looked like when it was vibrant and full of life, hopes, and dreams of the people living there. Although Flint may be but a shadow of its former self, I still think of it during better times. It's well worth the trip if you can get there, besides being a pipe haven, Danny and the rest of the staff are a wealth of information on all things pipe.

Jim and I also started going to J R Cigar in Southfield Michigan which is a suburb northwest of Detroit. J.R. Cigar is a real treat to visit. This particular store isn't all that big as far as pure size goes but it is a real tobacco shop. Like other tobacco emporiums the whole inside of the store is a humidor. Because of the cigar craze I started smoking a better class of cigars. Jim was a great educator on all aspects of a cigars, his number one rule was that if you were knowledgeable about the makings of and the different tobacco used to make a cigar, one did not need to spend a whole lot of money to get a very fine smoke.

The first time I went into J.R.'s there were overwhelming cigars stacked floor to ceiling. That was the first time I met Mary, she is extremely helpful to all that come into the store. In fact Mary sold me my first actual box of cigars I've ever bought, before this time I would buy a few at a time or in boxes of five. I must confess that I got caught up in the 90's cigar craze to an extent but I preferred a pipe. After visiting J. R.'s for the first time a week or so after that I had heard some of the guys I worked with talking about a place called Humidor One and Panache. It wasn't but seven miles from J.R.'s on 10 Mile Road and Evergreen also in Southfield, Michigan. With a short detour I could stop at these places on my way home from work if the traffic wasn't too bad. I say that because it took a damn good reason for me to stop anywhere on my way home from work. The sooner I could get back to the lake the better. I'd much rather be by the water than be inland.

The first time I went into Humidor One and Panache was a mind blowing experience, this place had everything tobacco you could dream of and then some. When you first walked in was the Panache part then turning left would take you into the tobacconist part of the store. On the Panache side Max's wife owned that part. There she sold high end luggage and brief cases and the like. Walking into the tobacco side you were greeted to a world of everything tobacco you could ever dream of. I was fortunate enough to meet Max Burns the owner, and his right hand men Shawn and Rick. To get into the humidor you stepped up and went thru an old door into a room that was around 30 by 50 feet. This humidor was packed with what looked like thousands upon thousands of boxes of cigars and bag on top of bag of their bulk pipe tobacco off in one corner. Exiting the humidor and walking ten feet or so then turning left you entered another room; there you were treated to a wonderland of all things pipe and the accouterments that go along with the fine art of pipe smoking and all the enjoyment as well. My first time in this room of pipe heaven I just stood there for quite some time taking it all in. I had been in more than a few pipe shops but this one really had a comfortable feel to it. This room also had a certain element of classiness to it that you felt more than saw. After standing there with a star struck look on my mug, Shawn came up and introduced himself to me. Pleasantries out of the way he asked if there was anything in particular that I had in mind. I admitted to Shawn that I wasn't all that knew to pipe smoking but I was overwhelmed by all the different types of pipe tobacco. Don't get me wrong; I had throughout the years picked up quite a bit of knowledge, but standing there talking to Shawn was a very enlightening conversation to say the least.

In this room were four or five different counters with jars and jars of pipe tobacco. I was ready to start taking the tops off all the jars to find out what might taste good. Shawn started explaining to me the different types of tobacco that went into the blends and the strait tobaccos. Man did I ever feel like an idiot. What I've always heard sure proved to be true, that just when you think you know something, you find out you know even less than you thought you knew. I spent more than an hour and a half talking to Shawn that day and came away with a wealth of knowledge that I didn't have before I walked in. While there I picked out a new pipe and some good English and Virginia blends that didn't bite at all.

Humidor One and Panache became one of my favorite tobacco shops. Not long after that Jim and I started to visit Campbell's Red Door Tobacco in East Lansing, Michigan. It's located right off of Grand River Avenue which is the main drag going right through Michigan State University Campus. Doug is the owner of Campbell's and still runs the shop along with Josh his right hand man. You can count on one of them being there all the time. This shop is long and narrow and you get that great personal warm tobacco shop feeling immediately as you enter this fine old shop. I'm taking it for granted that you know exactly what I'm talking about if you are reading this book. (By the way, Thank You fellow pipe smoker and reader)

Without a doubt Campbell's is one of the nicest most considerate shops that I've ever had the pleasure of patronizing. One can enter the shop from the front door on the street side or if you park in the lot behind you can walk in the back door. Walking in the front door there is a small table with a couple chairs that you can sit and enjoying your pipe or cigar and watch what was going on in the Campus.

Behind the table is a wall shelving unit that Doug displays the humidors they sell. Walking further in on the left are these rich looking old shelves lining the wall filled with tobacco and other related items. On the right are glass counter type display cases that are filled with pipes high end lighters and tampers. Behind the counter towards the front but still within reach for customers is the proverbial basket of pipes. This is not your ordinary run of the mill grade of basket pipe but something a bit more, some nice pipes can be found in that basket. Taking a few more steps in on the left is where Doug mixes the blends that you'll find in jars lining the shelves on that side. They have some very good house blends such as the 30th Anniversary along with their Christmas blends. Campbell's also carries Cornell & Diehl, Benjamin Hartwell and other quality brands of tinned tobacco. Turning to the right taking a few steps is the walk in humidor it's long and narrow and filled with all types of cigars. Whatever kind of cigar you're looking for can be found in their adequately sized space. From high end to middle of the road smokes. Jim and I have been in there more than once when a Professor would come in and purchase a cigar or two to smoke while they grade papers. Standing at the counter paying for your treasures and looking on the wall behind the counter you'll see a photograph of a late 70's model Maserati coup. I forgot the story behind the car but I'm quite sure Doug would be glad to tell you about it. All in all Campbell's Red Door is a true tobacconist shop. Just a block or two away on Grand River there is a place called The Curious Book shop which is worth the time to check out. Before I forget, one thing about the shop that cracks me up is the bathroom in the back of the store. This tiny room will defiantly take you back in time. I won't elaborate further on this space as it is something you have to experience firsthand as mere words do not do it justice.

I started collecting pipes and centered my attention on Free Hand pipes, they had character to them. While at Paul's one Saturday in the fall Jim, Paul, and Danny were discussing Ben Wade pipes, free hands in particular, Paul started pulling out these stately boxes of Ben Wade pipes with four to six in a display box. From that time on Ben Wade Free Hand has been my pipe of choice, I like all pipes but those are my favorites. I gravitate towards free hands of any brand but as with most of us I have a bit of an eclectic accumulation of different styles and types of pipes.

Sunday nights Jim and I would get together at his place and smoke a pipe-full of some new or interesting tobacco one of us found in our travels or if we happened upon a cigar that looked rich and promising we'd smoke that while watching 60 Minutes or listening to Garrison Keillor and The Prairie Home Companion. During the boating season I would take one of my boats to Jims, the off boating time was ok for smoking and getting projects done while catching up on all the reading I set aside to be enjoyed looking out over a frozen lake. One week we were kicked back smoking an English blend when I told Jim I wanted to start looking for a Church Warden pipe. Having the required knowledge and insight that all pipe men possess the conversation for the duration of that night turned respectfully to pipes, Church Wardens in particular.

You must remember that I was talking to Captain Jim, possessor of great tobacco knowledge and teacher. So Jim felt that in order to enjoy a Church Warden pipe one must know the legend behind the name. This is how I was enlightened, Legend has it that during Victorian Times not every town or village had a proper jail. There being no jail cells to keep the undesired law breakers in they became wards of the church. While at the church the Wardens of the Church would watch over them. The wardens would sit across from said undesirables and watch them. Doing this when smoking a regular pipe would interrupt the important view the Warden had over their subjects, so they started to lengthen their pipes so as not to muck up their view. It must have caught on quite well as Church Wardens are still available to this very day. Whether or not that is the true story behind that pipe I do not know as I tried to research these facts while writing this but it was to no avail, personally I prefer the church version as it conjures images of friar tuck type warden characters puffing on their long bent pipes watching over ruffians while nursing a tankard of ale by oil lamps and candle light in a Church built buy craftsman in the truest form.

Anyway the search being afoot I started stopping in every tobacco shop I could find in my travels in Michigan, Ohio, and Indiana those being the primary states of travel with my job at the time. After scoping out several pipes Jim and I would discuss these pipes on Sunday nights. This was no small quest mind you I kept searching for the perfect church warden wherever I looked, not a single pipe jumped out with that look and feel that you get when all the planets align and things are right with the world and deep down in your soul that you know this one pipe and it alone is the exact instrument that you've been on the hunt for, you start wondering how you got this far in life without it. Truth be told, I strongly suspect that all Brothers of the Pipe feel the same way or damn close to it whenever we see a new prospective pipe we must acquire.

The week after Thanksgiving that year I was on a run that took me to Youngstown, Ohio with 14 stops at G.M. dealerships that took 15 to 17 hours to complete usually putting me back to Livonia, Michigan around four o'clock in the afternoon, just in time for the mass panic of the multitudes trying to get out of the metro area. I referred to this madness as the speed, crawl, stop, speed, repeat, over and over, it never took much to trip the trigger to set this chain of events into motion. It could be anything from a bird sitting atop a mile post marker or some poor motorist with a flat, every single car truck whatever had to go like hell then come to a crawl then stop take a slow mental picture of the real or imagined distraction then haul ass again. I used to almost always volunteer for overtime thinking that I'd rather make some extra money than sit in traffic trying to get home. That week I wanted to stop at Humidor One later in the week so I started cutting time off my run so that if I got out of Livonia on time or even 20 to 30 minutes ahead of time and if everything went perfectly I could shave two and a half hours off my run, that would give me time to stop at Humidor One look at their Church Wardens and still beat the rush.

Arriving at the shop I told Shawn what I was in search of. We went back to the pipe room where Shawn showed me what they had. Not seeing one pipe I liked Shawn was honest enough to tell me that the church wardens pipes they had were not worth a shit. What a letdown after planning this for a week. He said that what I was looking for would most likely be found in a more predominant pipe shop. I bought some pipe tobacco and a few Sosa cigars and took off to beat the traffic.

Stopping by Jims before I got home we made plans to do a tobacco run the next day. We'd go to Campbell's in East Lansing then to Paul's in Flint, then top the day off by cruising down to J.R.'s in Southfield. Jim had a few weeks earlier purchased a 1978 Silver Anniversary Edition Corvette that he had been admiring for a few years, so after checking the weather channel we decided to take the Vette. Going on a 200 hundred mile tobacco run in a Corvette was our idea of a good time. The next day was a tad chilly but we popped the T-Tops off anyway and turned the heater on full blast and we were off on our monthly mission of searching for all things new or old in the shops of our favorite tobacconist.

Arriving at Doug's place (Campbell's) we sat and chewed the fat with Doug while solving most of the world's problems in a matter of 20 minutes or so the conversation got to the more important mission at hand to find the perfect church warden. After discussing said pipe and what shape and character I was looking for Jim pipe's up (no pun intended but it does sound good doesn't it) an says you need a real proper warden with oomph and oompaha to it, not one of these cheap imposters. Jim takes out his Cross Pen and sketches a drawing of a pipe that was long and dropped down a lot more than just jutting out with just a little bend to it. Doug takes a long look at the drawing and admits he has nothing in the shop that comes close. We all looked at each other and said Paul's at the same time, after getting a chuckle out of that Jim and I started doing our other shopping. Jim picked out his usual pound and a half of 25th Anniversary, the same weight with the 1980 Christmas Blend. I picked out some of the same along with a tin or two to try out on some of our Sunday night smoke sessions. We never ever went into a tobacconist shop without buying something as we are fortunate that they are in business to supply the tools of our most sacred hobby. So after putting the T-tops back on the Vette we were off to the truest pipe shop within our allotted distance at that time besides being the 2nd stop on our list anyway. We had a great cruise over to Flint, smoking our newly purchased tobacco and talking about the pipes and different types of tobacco we had observed at Doug's. Both of us knew I'd wind up buying a church warden from Paul but his prices were a bit higher than most. But then again the quality you find there is hard to find elsewhere.

The best way to explain that visit to Paul's is the scene from the first Harry Potter movie when Hagrid took Harry to Olivanders Wand Shop. That movie didn't come out until 2003 or so but when I watched that scene it was very similar to that day at Paul's. We went and told the wizard himself (Paul) what we were in search of. Paul the wise Wizard stood behind the left side pipe counter contemplating and considering what I was telling him. After a few moments Paul turns with a concerned look on his face as his hands are rubbing together as if he's up to something. He walked half way down the counter and opened a long drawer, pulled out a dozen or so boxes, set them aside and got to the objects of his search. Paul the Wizard picked a couple of long kewl looking boxes within which rested pipes that were definably great pipe's but still did not have the character I was after. Well this had Paul puzzled for a moment, and then he started looking deeper into the many nooks and crannies in the shop, after looking at quite a few pipes and still not finding THE pipe. All of a sudden Paul gets this gleam in his eyes and wanders off to the front left corner takes a couple steps up this ladder reaches way up into this higher cabinet and pulled out a long brown box that had Clairmont in a gold script written on the top of the box. It felt as if I was having a metaphysical moment just looking at the box. Paul set the box on the counter and slowly lifted the top off. Inside there was a long dark green velvet pipe sleeve with the gold Clairmont script on it also. Picking up the sleeve Paul started to pull the pipe out, even before it was all the way out I knew without doubt that this was the pipe I had been in search of. He kept pulling it out for what seemed like 10 seconds, now this pipe was loaded with character. The pipe looked great, it's a real sitting pipe as it is ten and a half inches long, the end of the mouth piece is shaped like that of a Peterson Pipe except the air hole comes straight out of the end instead of on top. The bit drops down to the shank that looks like the shape of one of those types of pipe's that just about drops right down then makes a U turn so the bowl is in the upright position like with a regular sized pipe only this pipe looked as if it were on steroids. Paul handed me the pipe and I started to examine it. I'm sure you've all got that feeling when you pick up a pipe for the first time and it just feels perfect in your hand, that's the moment when you just know without a doubt that this pipe must be in your collection. Everything about this pipe seems to be in harmony with itself and all things surrounding it (especially me). Jim gave it his nod of approval and that was that. After that Jim and I split a pound of Paul's triple vanilla and some others of Paul's special blends. While I was piling stuff on the counter there was a display on top of the humidor display case that had a cardboard presentation from Amphora for a tinned blend named

Cesare Borgia that came in a very cool blue tin. Besides it was advertised for fifty percent off, not being one to turn down a good deal I bought a couple tins and really didn't give it much thought as to what it would taste like as the tin alone had an old time pipe look to it that would make anyone's pipe area look better for it.

Stepping out to the Vette Jim asked if I wanted to drive thinking that I would rather scope out my new pipe than drive his car. I fooled him by giving him my bag of personal enjoyment just purchased and grabbing the keys. Jim just stood there opened mouth with a blank look on his face and I said, come on lets go we're burnin daylight.

Next stop was J.R.s, a bit of a hop down I-75 to Square Lake Road to Telegraph South 8 miles then West on Twelve Mile then hang a Michigan U turn heading South on Northwestern Hwy. Two blocks and bingo you're turning into J.R's parking lot. On the way south Jim pulled out my new church warden and started inspecting it with a keen eye. From the lip to the mortise joint is seven and a half inches; to the bottom is ten and a half inches so it's a longish pipe. Coming down the back of the pipe the pattern in the briar splits so that there's a tight burl pattern on right side then on the left it goes into a starburst of strait grain. It has a green dot on the front of the stem in front, on the back there are three numbers stamped upside down 019 what meaning this has I have no idea. Maybe someone more knowledgeable than me can email me with more info. Below that spelled right-side up is the word ITALY below that Handmade, then below the words Leisure Line, Leisure being on top. On the left hand side Clairmont is written in script.

Years later when I watched the first Harry Potter movie when Harry was in the Wand Shop was a lot like being in Paul's that day especially when the wise old wizard is talking to himself saying, I wonder if this one will work as he gives each wand to Harry to try out then he talks to himself again as he picks out the only wand among thousands that he thinks will do the right trick. Harry picks up the wand and gets a magical glow about him and the wise wizard is just as pleased as Harry. On top of that I didn't have to fly a broom to Southfield but got to drive a vintage Vette to our next tobacco shop on the list for the day. When we got to J.R'.s I took it in to show the staff what I just bought as by that time Jim and I were getting to know them on a first name basis. Everyone there all agreed it was a very proper Church Warden especially since it was purchased at Paul's as his is a well-respected shop. After everyone had a good going over on the pipe we got some of J.R.'s special coffee they sell and started cruising the store for whatever cigars we had in mind to get that day. We usually got to J.R'.s once a month so Jim really stocks up when we are there. I'd buy a box of whatever was our cigar of choice then pick out some five packs and or a couple of single cigars that looked and felt worthy of trying, one never knows what one may stumble across in the search for the perfect smoke. I was once in a discount tobacco store around this time while I was doing a route in northern Indiana that had a sale on Maduro Coronas with Burt Reynolds name on the wrapper, I asked the girl why they were so cheap and was told that for some unknown reason people were just not buying them. Just down the street I had just made my last stop for the day so I slit the end and lit up right there. This cigar was great, I mean really great as in fine. They were on sale for twenty dollars a box. I bought 2 boxes that day and learned that Tobacco Joe's had multiple locations in the area I was in. Over the next few months I must have bought a dozen boxes, most were given away or traded for pipes.

On this particular day I picked out a couple of J.R's Ultimate's in a 52 x 7 size to smoke on one of our Sunday Night smoke fests. For some reason I was unaware of at the time they also had Cesare Borgia on sale, I don't remember why but some little voice told me to buy some more, I just bought some at Paul's but there tins were cheaper yet so I bought 4 more. Depleting each of our allotted expendable tobacco money we headed back to Howell.

The Friday before Christmas that year I planned my route just right and got off early so I swung by J.R.'s to wish Mary and the rest of the crew Merry Christmas, then I went to Humidor One to do the same there. While there talking to Shawn in the pipe room I was checking out the basket pipes then under the glass counter top I spied a unique looking pipe in the case below. Shawn pulled it out of the case so I could take a better look at it. This pipe was not the usual style of pipe for me as it was a semi bent billard in the standard shape but it was the rim of the pipe that set it apart from the dozens of others resting along with it in the case. The stain was a bit dark with a nice grain to the bowl and shank. On top of the rim it had these deep grooves cut into it that were stained black the stem was acrylic that did a good job of complementing the rest of the pipe. All the different aspects of this pipe seemed to be in perfect harmony which made this quite a good looking pipe. I wanted this pipe but when I looked down at the box it came out of and observed the price I was taken back a bit. I looked at Shawn and handed the pipe back to him as this was way beyond my budget especially during the Christmas Holidays and the big day being less than a week away. Although it was out of my price range at that time I asked Shawn if he'd set it aside for me. He bent down and grabbed the box put the pipe in it, put the lid on it then tossed it into the basket of pipes on the counter. Looking at Shawn he said according to law the pipe he just tossed into the basket must be sold for the price marked on said basket which was $29.99. Wow what a deal, a Stanwell pipe for that price was great, Shawn said Merry Christmas with a grin on his face then he grabbed a tin of Cesare Borgia telling me that I might like this blend. As with the other shops I had been to in the past month they too had it on sale. Not giving the tobacco much thought I paid for everything and bid everyone a good night and tried to beat the rush hour home.

After getting on the road I was handling my new Stanwell with an appreciating eye, I couldn't wait to smoke this pipe. Taking Shawn's advice I popped open the tin of Cesare Borgia and loaded up, I hadn't opened any of the other Borgia tins I had bought lately so I didn't know what to expect when I opened it. Lifting the lid off and folding the foil wrap back I was hit with a very different aroma than the usual run of the mill tined aromatic blends that I was accustomed to. The aroma was very rich with a hint of something like cloves but not quite that strong of a note, it could easily be mistaken for any combination of casing infused within it. Loading my newest pipe acquisition the aroma of the tobacco filled the cab of my pickup with the fragrance of a soon to be enjoyable bowl of tobacco. That day it seemed like all of the Metro Detroit people got it in their feeble minds to leave town at the same time. I had just started puffing away when the traffic started its usual stop and go all the way back to Howell which gave me more time to appreciate my smoke. The Stanwell smoked great and the tobacco was excellent. I could never put my finger on what it was that made this blend so good but to me it was great. This was turning out to be a good day as this new blend tasted great. That Sunday at Jims I told him to try this Cesare blend, he wasn't as impressed with it as I was but that's just the way it goes and why there are so many different blends available. After Christmas Jim and I made another trip to Paul's, I wanted to pick up some more Cesare Borgia tobacco if it was still on sale. Once inside Paul's I asked Danny why this tobacco was on sale in most shops I frequented. Danny told me that the company Amphora was not going to import it anymore. That's just great, I find a blend that fits all my personal tastes and now they aren't importing it in the future. I bought most of what they had on the shelf then asked Paul if he could save the rest of what was in the store for me to purchase at another time. Paul also told me if worse came to worse he could make up a blend that was just like or pretty close to it.

Jim and I had joined the Arrowhead Pipe Club at Paul's and started going to the once a month meetings held at the shop. Attending the meetings I met a longtime friend of Jims named Jerry McGuire he worked as a supervisor at one of the GM plants in the area. One Saturday Jim and I made a stop at Jerry's house on the way to Paul's. Jerry wanted to show off his new house and his pipe collection. Jim told me that the two of them used to talk a lot about pipes and cigars while working together when they got a break from watching over the questionable antics of the UAW workers that were there to work but for some unknown explanation known only to them which rumor has it that UAW meant Unable to Work instead of the United Auto Workers Union. (I'll get more into the UAW in my next book as I have had dealings with them for 30 plus years)

Jerry's place was a real show piece, it was a fairly new house built maybe 5 years earlier. Along with the house Jerry had two or three acres of land. I call anyone that owns more than a city lot a land baron. Jerry being the gracious land baron host that he was gave us the grand tour of the house and grounds then it was time to get down to the serious business of gawking at his pipe collection. To be more precise this part of the tour was more like looking through a museum with collections plural instead of singular as in just one. Jerry has one hell of a collection that's taken many years and many miles to accumulate. Like many other pipe smokers in the world Jerry is a fan of any and all things Sherlockian. He has a couple of curio cabinets displaying an enormous collection of just about anything Sherlock Holmes. He even has all the Basil Rathbone Sherlock movies. I had never seen a private collection so vast; to look at all his pipes would have taken much more time than we had allowed for.

Jerry and his wife spent many vacations wondering around flea markets in several states, Jerry looking for pipes and such while his wife went about collecting her cherished keep sakes. In my travels around the country many years after I met Jerry I too started checking out flea markets and the like, I was never as lucky as Jerry in finding the Dunhill in a basket luck. But there was a time I went to a flea market in Quartzite, Arizona and found this huge mug shaped like Sherlock's head that was stuffed with a dozen pipes of the drug store variety. I didn't want the pipes but the mug was pretty cool so I bought the bunch and put it in storage when I got back to Michigan not giving it another thought for a few years. (More on this particular bunch of pipes later)

That winter I won the Arrowhead Pipe Club Smoking Contest then came in second in the Michigan contest held in the spring. Sometimes I do very well other times not so well, I always smoke the same pipe it's a bent egg shape with the bottom flattened so it sits upright. It's also one of Paul's Pipe Shop Cuyahoga Pipes. That's Paul's special shop brand that he treats with a decade old secret recipe that he treats the inside of the bowls with. I've had a few of these pipes and all are excellent smokers. Besides being fun and interesting, talking with other pipe smokers these contests gave people access to pipe traders and venders alike.

A few things came to my attention during the cigar craze, the startup and sudden arrival of mini cigar and cigarette stores in every other strip mall in the country. It was hilarious observing some of the workers and owners. They were damn sure proud of their inventory. One afternoon on my way home from work I stopped into one of these shops as I wanted a cigar to smoke on the way home, I had my pipe but I was in the mood for a nice dark Maduro Corona for the ride home. I walked into their small humidor and in walked this guy behind me. Standing there looking for what I wanted the guy starts up a conversation with me about the fine selection of smokes they had on hand. He asked me if I had a favorite cigar.

No I said, I prefer to keep my options open and stay on a never ending quest to find better and more interesting tobacco than limit myself to a single brand or type. He looked at me for a moment at a loss for words then he says.

Oh I've picked out my cigar and it's been rated by Cigar Aficionado. He puffs up his chest as if he just discovered something of great historical meaning. The way this guy was dressed and the cut of him he looked like a typical middle management type that seems to always be in some ones way.

I said, well damn that's great, then he picked out a natural wrapper cigar of a reputable brand and exclaims with great pride and wisdom that this was his prized cigar. This cigar he had in hand I have had experience with and it's a good smoke. Six months earlier Cigar Aficionado had in fact did give this particular cigar a good rating then the price skyrocketed, he was going to pay $12.95 for a cigar that prior to being rated sold for $3.95.

I looked at the cigar then him and said, yes a fine choice you made. He did an about face and left. It never ceased to amaze me at the gullibility of some people. Most all the cigar smokers of that time don't seem to be enjoying cigars anymore. The same holds true with most of the pop up cigar-cigarette stores. We did get a few good things out of that boom; I feel there are more people interested in pipes than before the boom. Pipe's and Tobacco magazine was born and is still with us today. There have been a few good books written about the hobby that I'll get into later.

Getting back to the guy in the store, it's the poor schmucks that don't take the time to understand the building of a cigar or a certain pipe tobacco blend. This type of individual thought that the more they spent and if they had seen a certain advertisement that rang a bell with them they knew in their deep other worldly wisdom that they were getting the very best. Like the old saying goes; never judge a book by its cover. Besides what is it they say, what is isn't and what isn't is. This holds true in many things. I had a nice woodshop in my garage that was my haven. After reading about how some pipe smokers played around with tobacco to get unique homemade blends I started doing the same. I have this nice machete knife that I keep as Sharpe as a razor that I would use to cut and blend the different tobaccos I was starting to accumulate. This was starting to be real fun besides the extra good mixes I was making and spending more time in my shop, the bags and tins of these ingenious blends went in a special place for aging.

During that spring and summer I was in search of a 70's vintage Corvette, it took a few months but I finally found one in Flint, Michigan at a dealer that sold sports and muscle cars. It wasn't by design or a grand plan but I found a 1978 Silver Anniversary L-82 Corvette with an oyster leather interior. This car was clean for its age. The only difference between my car and Jim's was that he had wider tire's than I did. They also had a 1966 series 2 Jaguar E-Type that I fell in love with that day also but the price tag was a bit much considering the overall condition of the car. It was a drop top in a very ugly off white color, I still think of that car to this day along with every other E-Type I've ever laid eyes on.

After that Jim and I would take both Vette's on our tobacco journeys. There was one Saturday in particular that stands out over most of the other tobacco runs we went on during the boom days. We heard about a newer tobacconist shop in Orchard Lake, Michigan. Somewhere between 14 Mile Road. and Maple Road, It being a nice day for a cruise we took the back roads to Orchard Lake Road heading south, we found the shop on the west side of the road in an upper scale strip mall. I mention that as this area is an affluent section of the Northwest Metro area.

Upon arrival we found places to park right in front of the shop. Walking in I didn't get that warm cozy feeling one gets when they walk into a friendly tobacconist shop. This store had a sterol feel to it, keeping an open mind we started looking around. Everything in the shop seemed like it was marked up 25% higher compared to other shops I had been in. We started looking around at the selection of pipes and were soon confronted with a pushy sales clerk that had quite the haughty attitude. All of a sudden I didn't feel welcome in this shop at all. This saleswoman thought she knew everything and then some. She was maybe 32 to 36 years old. Judging by her tone of voice she came across as a real pain in the ass. I knew this was going to be fun as Jim got that look in his eye he gets when he's going to play with someone's brain or should I say what they understand as their brain.

Jim must have been giving this considerable thought as he didn't say anything right away. We continued our tour to the back where the walk-in humidor was. Jim had lit up one of his bigger cigars a half hour earlier and still had about 45 minutes left of smoking left on it. After walking into the humidor Miss Bitch came barging in and told Jim under no circumstances was he allowed to smoke in there exquisite humidor.

Giving her a look we looked at each other then back at her, she was turning many shades of red and I figured steam would start coming out of different parts of her head. Then she started scolding Jim for even smoking a cigar in the new store period. This nut case was on the verge of blowing a real mental gasket to the point of being scary. We started to walk out and she just could not keep her yap shut about Jim's cigar. Jim turned and asked her a fairly easy cigar question that we both knew she couldn't answer. She stood there with her mouth moving up and down in slow motion but no sound was coming out. I was thinking right then that maybe we should vacate this haughty shop of turds and get out of dodge. Grabbing Jim by the sleeve I did my best to usher him out the door before he or I said something that we might for some reason regret later.

Once outside the shop I turned and looked back into the store. There she stood glaring at us like we had just violated some heavenly golden rule that she and she alone knew about. I looked back at Jim and said: what's that old saying, you can pour all the perfume you want onto a pig but no matter what it is still a pig. This person reminded me of that.

Having escaped the psycho pig bitch we made a bee line to J.R.'s which was only a few miles away, knowing that we were welcome there smoking or not. We walked in the door and Jim spotted Mary and asked her if he could smoke in the store as the whole store was a humidor. Mary looked at Jim as if he had just landed from another planet, which in a matter of speaking we had done just that very thing. Walking towards Mary I said everyone gather round you've got to hear this. After telling the crew and a few customers about our other planetary experience up the road everyone got a good laugh and another guy said that his wife stopped in that store the previous week and she didn't even stay long enough to pick up his pipe tobacco as she also was treated like something other than human. After that Mary told us we had gotten our just rewards because we dared visit that evil place. Everyone agreed to never patronize that shop ever again, which calmed Mary down. I wanted to talk Mary into giving that girl her come unpins but being the fiery redhead Mary is that would have been an unfair thing to do even though said entity was a real bitch, she would have been nothing but a snack for our Mary.

After visiting with the kind folks and customers at J.R.'s Jim led the way to a drive in out in Dexter Michigan via back roads I never knew existed, one thing I could count on was that I knew Jim would never take me down any dirt roads as he didn't wish to get his dressed tires dusty either. In Dexter we grabbed a burger and a shake then took the long way back to Howell which took us right through Hell Michigan yes there really is a Hell, Michigan. I never gave it any thought until now but we must have looked rather peculiar cruising the back roads in identical Corvettes smoking our pipes and cigars.

Leaving Hell that day Jim led the way to Brighton. Michigan where the United Street Machine Association was having a car show. Jim used to be a fulltime judge at these events but at this time he was taking a break. We started busting chops with the multitude of Hot Rodders while smoking a couple of our recently acquired cigars. Taking off from there driving west on Grand River we came upon a group of 30 Corvettes having some type of meet in the parking lot. Of course we had to check it out so we pulled in and parked close to the action. This Corvette meet was put on by a sub-chapter of a chapter of some Corvette Club that we had heard of but had no intention of ever joining. Our idea of enjoying our Vette's was to DRIVE them not sit on a tarmac someplace in a folding chair on a Saturday afternoon. Looking at some of these cars I observed a few of these guys with Q-tips detailing the tread on their tires. I admit I am a certifiable detail nut when it comes to anything I drive but this bunch was taking it to a level that seemed to me to take up all of my driving time, leaving me with a spotless car but no time to drive it.

As I always did when I saw another Vette with aluminum wheels I look to see what kind of shine they had to them, 95% of the time they were dull and looked like shit. To give you a better idea of our arrival, Jim and I both had chambered exhaust that was music to our ears but quite possibly could be mistaken for noise pollution by some inhabanits of this planet. Never could figure out why the sound of a perfectly tuned American V-8 with a bit of cam to it didn't tickle other people as it did me. Anyway upon our arrival we had everyone's attention because we were tuned loud and our cars looked like we could just pull up and inter the show. Besides I had spent a lot of time polishing both sets of wheels to make them shine better than chrome. That alone was a big attention getter. Walking around the cars we got some dirty looks from some people for smoking a cigar, while others asked how we got our wheels to shine like they did. Some of these cars had serious work done to them such as turbo's, multiple carbs, headers and the like. There was a 78 Silver Anniversary with a nice Phase III Cowl induction hood that looked great, when I looked under the hood the engine looked terrible. He had not paid any attention to the engine or the engine compartment. I spoke to the owner, he had found the car behind someone's garage with little critters living in it. Looking at the before pictures laying on the dash and comparing those against the car before me was amazing considering he only had one day a week to work on it. He started asking about our rides and wanted desperately to know how we got our wheels so shiny, usually I just told people we did it with metal polish and left it at that. This guy was putting so much work into his Vette that I explained to him the proper way to polish aluminum. I gave him my phone number and told him some weekend we could get together and I would let him use my compounds and buffer. A few weeks before this Jim and I had put a Chevy ZZ 4 crate motor in my car as the old one was really lacking in the shit and grit department. After telling him about the fine points of a factory made performance crate motor available through your local G.M. dealer he wanted to see my engine bay so we walked over to our cars so he could take a look. On our way to my ride he asked about the cigars we were smoking and yes he was a fellow brother of the tobacco leaf. Upon reaching our cars Jim pulled a couple of smokes out of one of the boxes he'd just bought and gave them to him and I did the same. After admiring our cars for a bit I noticed the wind coming up and told Jim we should get back to my place as it was shaping up to be a nice afternoon for a sail.

We bid our new friend a farewell and high tailed it out of there. Leaving the lot turning west onto Grand River again I couldn't help myself so I grabbed first and stepped on it rather hard for a few moments, that's all it took for my new 400 pony's to kick in and break loose the tires, drive it like you stole it has been my motto on more than one occasion and this time was no different. After getting straightened out I hit second and the ass end came out so I backed out of it to regain control. I could just imagine the looks on the faces of the parking lot queen car owners, faces as we took off. I've always believed that driving or operating something was more fun than just looking at it. If you don't use it you could lose it right?

The same holds true for your women, treat them like a thoroughbred and they won't turn into an old nag.

That fall Pipe's and Tobacco magazine asked its readership to send in articles that were of interest to pipe smokers. I've always wanted to write so I took my miniature tape recorder and camera, called ahead to make sure Paul was going to be there and went to his shop to interview him.

When I got to Paul's we settled into some nice arm chairs between the store and the pipe hospital where Paul reminisced about his life in the pipe industry. He had even been to Hollywood to teach some actors and actresses how to smoke a pipe; Greta Garbow was one that comes to mind. I filled up 4 mini cassettes listening to Paul recount his life history. Paul is a bit of Jimmy Stewart, Henry Fonda, James Cagney and John Wayne all rolled into one person. Sitting there hearing Paul recount the good old days of pipe's it seemed like I was in some kind of trance. After we had finished and I put my notes away we went back into the store and I started talking to one of Paul's staff about what they smoked.

Most tobacconist shop's I've been to, more than a few times always have a couple of guy's that hang around and step in to help when needed. Paul's was no exception; Greg came to every pipe club meeting, event, and preferred hanging out at Paul's instead of the local watering hole. When Paul and I came back into the store he was weighing out some pipe tobacco for a few customers. I waited till he was done with the patrons and we started talking as he cleaned the counter off. After he had all the loose tobacco on the counter gathered into a pile he went to his coat and pulled out a good sized zip lock baggy then came back to the counter and swept all the extra into the zip lock telling me that this was his own recipe for his personal blend which he fittingly called; Paul's Counter Top Blend never to be repeated twice. He put some in a baggy for me to try. It was a really good smoke, so from then on whenever Greg had some extra he would give me some. More times than not the Counter Top Blend turned out to be some very good stuff. Jim even agreed most of it was exceptional.

During that visit I took a lot of pictures of Paul, Danny, and the shop to go along with the article. That weekend I started writing. At first it wasn't turning out that good as I hadn't done any writing since I left the east coast when I would make notes of the adventures I was having. I've been doing that since I first started trucking over the road I always wanted to write a book or two about my adventures and misadventures over the years. Then all of sudden after walking away from it for a few days, bang it just came to me and I started writing. The article turned out pretty good judging by the response I got from Paul and others in the club, I gave Paul a copy which he framed and put on the wall. I sent the article and pictures into Pipes and Tobacco magazine then never heard from them.

A funny thing happened with that article a couple years later. The yearly pipe contest and swap meet was held in Flint, Michigan that year and upon my arrival Paul introduced me to a woman that was a writer for Pipe's and Tobacco magazine. That year I didn't do very well in the contest but found a few pipe's to buy. I found out that after the show Paul and his son Danny took her back to the pipe shop and showed her the article I wrote. Then a few months after that her article came out in the magazine and it was almost a word for word copy of my article. I didn't think too much of the writer woman when I met her and even less after the piece came out in Pipe's magazine. I shrugged it off. The important thing to me was that Paul got to be in the magazine. I've still got a copy or two of the article I wrote, while writing this I started looking for it but to no avail, it's most likely in one of my storage lockers which at this time I haven't been able to find, but when I do I'll update this book so you can read it and compare mine to hers. It would be very interesting to find out what you think.

As the 90's came to an end and everyone seemed to be worried about Y2K and the effects it would have on the world and what not I didn't think too much about it until my company switched from daytime dealer delivery to night delivery. I hadn't worked nights in quite a while but it didn't take long to get back in the groove. Spending as much time behind the wheel as I have during my life radio is a big part of my life and watching Good Morning America in the morning when I got home from work before I hit the sack was just about the only news I got.

I started listening to the Art Bell Radio show at night. He and his guests started talking about Y2K as if it was the end of life as we knew it. Maybe a little history of Art Bell is in order here. Art is a radio talk show guy located in Pahrump, Nevada and talks quite a bit about aliens, and just about anything else the normal people of the world think of as unusual. That's not the case with Art as his show might be a tad out there at times but it is always entertaining to say the least. Well, after hearing all of this talk I too got caught up in the hoop-a-la of it all. Jim and I had many conversations on this topic during our Sunday night smoking ritual. Jim was of the opinion that getting a generator would be a good thing to have, since we lost power quite often during windy storms. Having extra food, water, batteries, and candles should be stocked up on just in case, was our train of thought. A week or so after it turned 1999 we had a storm come through that nocked the power out on a Saturday night on my end of the lake. I had already begun stocking up on candles so I lit something like 30 of them throughout the cottage. The next morning Jim came over with another box just in case I ran out. Being home alone that morning Jim and I lit up a couple of cigars and started talking about how efficient the candles were keeping the place warm and looking out over the lake. My dad showed up 30 minutes later, he had heard on the local radio station that parts of the lake were out of power so he wanted to check and see if things were ok. Dad had stopped smoking pipes and cigars the previous year but whenever he came over he would comment on how good our smokes smelled. Whenever dad came over and went someplace else people would always ask him if he had been to my place as he would have the fine aroma of great smokes about him.

Anyway, actually being without power for the better part of Sunday, that night at Jims we started rethinking our Y2K preparations as we had not discussed stocking up on tobacco. Yes, that was a shock to us too, being brothers of the pipe that should have been our first concern. We started making a plan as to where and how much to stock up on. This gave us a bonified reason to visit our tobacconist shops more often than before. We came across some good deals that year as the cigar boom seemed to be winding down. That was fine by us because it brought the prices down to a more reasonable cost.

Having listened to Art Bell for all that time during the run up to Y2K, and having taken most every precaution to get ready, it came and went without so much as a hiccup. Well, at least we were ready in case something did happen.

For the next year and a half life on the lake went along smoothly. Yes you guessed it 9/11 happened. I got home from work that day at 7:00 in the morning, after taking my Golden Retriever Chelsea for our ritualistic morning pontoon ride around the lake and letting her swim at the island for a bit we went back to the house and fixed something to eat. I had just cleaned up the kitchen and settled down on the couch to smoke my pipe and watch GMA as it was a beautiful sunny morning. While watching GMA they broke in with the story and film footage of The World Trade Center that apparently had been hit by a plane. Damn I thought this is bad, then the phone rang, it was my neighbor Henry Staron's wife Kathy.

Dave, turn on the news, she said. I told her I was watching it. We were on the phone talking watching it unfold when the second plane hit. Neither of us said anything for what seemed like minutes but in reality it was only seconds. Then the speculation started as to the country being under attack. I got off the phone and made a few calls then called Kathy back and asked her to knock on the door if anything else bad happened. After sleeping for a few hours I got up and let Chelsea out then Kathy came outside and told me the Pentagon had also been hit by a plane and of the other one crashing. I knew without a doubt that our country would never be the same and how right I was.

CHAPTER VII

BACK ON THE ROAD AGAIN

During this time my company went out of business, after that happened I was looking for work in places where I could remain a teamster but that didn't turn out so well. Having split up with my wife I thought I'd go back on the road thinking I could make a better income that way as opposed to driving local. I went to work at a company hauling freight regionally. Man, talk about boring, this was the pits all I did was go back and forth to the same old places again and again. I felt like a yo-yo on a string, it didn't take long for me to get out of there. A friend of mine told me that a car hauling company in Lansing, Michigan was hiring. That sounded great to me as I could be in the teamsters again.

I got hired there and moved to that area. After going through their instruction period where they teach you how to load and unload the cars I was back on nights again. Campbell's Red Door became my staple Tobacconist. I started increasing my eclectic collection and trying a host of new blends. During this time I began smoking quite a few non-aromatics. I was fairly familiar with English blends so trying different natural blends became interesting. It didn't take long before I started sharpening my taste buds in different tobacco. Besides being more acutely aware of the many blends available this became another fine search that to this day I'm still perusing with the same passion.

I sure thought hauling cars would be more exciting than what it was turning out to be. Don't get me wrong, putting the cars on the rig and figuring out how to load them using the dozens upon dozens of different configurations for the many decks you controlled with the hydraulics was great fun. Working nights again took a bit of an adjustment but after that it I was back in the Vampire community of night workers.

After doing this for a year I was watching television one morning before I hit the sack. A car commercial came on and if you've ever noticed the scenery where their filming the vehicle is always very unique and beautiful. To me these different locations all over the country looked more than interesting, I was curious to find out how the cars and trucks got to those locations. Needless to say I was upon another quest.

I started talking to some of the more savvy drivers I worked with, picking their brains for any shred of information leading me to different companies that did that type work and where they were located. After searching for a while I had a list of companies and started putting in applications to the ones I wanted to work for. That was easier said than done but I kept pursuing and won out in the end and went to work for a company located in Romulus, Michigan. Being that close to most of Ford Motor Company they did most of their work for them. Employed by this company I started traveling to places all over the country.

Learning all the ins and outs of readying a vehicle for photo shoots, commercials, television, movies, and car shows was a real gas. I had no idea of the many different types of film work and photos that went into making these events happen. We had a warehouse, yard, workshop, and photo studio in Palm Springs, California that I spent a lot of time at, as you all know most of the studios are in southern California. I worked with some talented people that could build a car out of a tin can. None of the people there smoked a cigar let alone a pipe; they smoked like a chimney but only cigarettes. We couldn't smoke in any of our shops but on the grounds we could.

When I wasn't on the road taking vehicles to locations and doing the car prep and hanging cameras all over the vehicles, I would be working in our Michigan or Palm Springs facilities. That meant you needed tools and lots of them. Say if two guys were getting ready to take a few vehicles to a photo or film shoot, we would do most of the prep work in our shops but you still needed 70% of your tools with you on location, as you needed to be ready to do whatever the producers or the manufacturer wanted you to do in order to get the perfect shot. Sometimes it took considerable planning to get the vehicles and your tools and all the other stuff you would need on any particular shoot. Such as different tires and wheels, seats, dashboards, etc. every shoot was different. We needed specialty tools to take out interiors and switch to a different color or whatever. If at all possible this was all loaded onto one trailer.

This was an added benefit for me as I love tools and what can be accomplished with the proper tools for whatever task you have at hand. What's that old saying, (you can never have enough money, tobacco, sex, or tools) now that I'm getting older I'm learning that the other old saying also holds true the older I get that number one never pass up a bathroom, number two never waste a hard on, and number three never trust a fart. If you're too young to understand that just wait your time will come. The tool venders such as Snap On, Mac, Matco, and others came in both shops every week. So you could add to your inventory of personal tools. Along with loading the cars we had to load our tools. I never showed up on location without the right tools to do the job I learned quickly that the last thing you wanted to do was tell the film people no. These people were all about anything is possible and you'd damn sure better be on board with them or else.

The first film shoot I was on they flew me out to Palm Springs to meet up with another guy then load two pickups and all the other parts, gear, and tools onto a 53 foot trailer. Having accomplished that we took off for Castaic, California, which is located 40 or so miles north of Los Angeles the south end of the Grapevine Mountain Range that takes you up four thousand plus feet and travel that about 80 miles and you would drop into the Emerald Valley on the north side.

This was the first time I had been back in California since I left the west coast. Castaic used to be one of my main stops after loading out of the Los Angeles basin and pointing my rig north. After maneuvering through the traffic and surviving the mine field they call a truck route and before heading up the Grapevine which is a 27 mile hard grade that's six percent grade. Stopping in Castaic after a long day of L.A. driving was a welcome stop as once I started up the grade I wouldn't stop for another 150 miles. There were good fuel stops there and as a welcome bonus the showers were nice.

The guy I was doing this shoot with was named Steve; he really knew what he was doing. After fueling our rig and doing an inspection on it we went down the street and checked into a Motel as we were going to be there for a few days. With the rest of that day to myself I walked up the street to see how much things had changed. My fuel stop that was on the west side of the street 16 years ago was not there. In its place a fenced in parking lot, but on the east side there was a new Pilot Truck Stop that was nice. Walking back to the motel I happened upon a chrome shop, uh oh. In the past when I drove over the road these places were known to alleviate me of many a hard earned dollar. I remember buying chrome for my truck instead of eating. An addiction to chrome can be a costly habit. On the plus side of this affliction your truck just keeps looking better; I'd even go so far as to say the performance improved too. The trouble with that last one is that nobody else could understand that unless you were a fellow chrome junky. The call time for the next morning was at 5:00 a.m. we left Castaic and headed east out of town and up another mountain then traveling a ways we turned into a driveway then wound our way to the top of a bluff to a church set in a most breathtaking view of a lake and the surrounding mountains. The sun was just coming up when we positioned our rig so we could access whatever we might need after unloading the pickup trucks. Being the first morning of the shoot it was a bit hectic for a while, but once the film crew informed us of the itinerary for the day and having that ready Steve said Ok let's go eat.

Like where I asked, we're on top of a mountain in a church parking lot and town is 20 miles from here.

Follow me rookie, he said. We started walking around the grip trucks and other film trailers and there sat a catering truck.

Well I thought, a roach coach is better than nothing. I asked Steve where the menu was. He explained to me then before I made ass out of myself that these gigs were always catered and that this was like a four star restaurant on wheels. Just walk up there and order whatever it is you want they can make anything. Looking around at some of the film crew eating I noticed what was on their plates looked good. I ordered a deluxe omelet. Wow, this was great I could definitely get used to this.

The commercial we were shooting was for Ford Trucks, the first part of the shoot was shot a couple miles east of the church. They had three or four camera cars following a Ford, Chevy, and Dodge pickup pulling different types of trailers up the hill. Toby Keith was a spokesman for Ford Truck at the time, the second part of the commercial would be shot in Norman, Oklahoma at Toby Keith's ranch. Rumor had it that he had just returned from the Bahamas after taking a break from doing a tour or movie and he didn't want to come out to California so we would take the show to him. He just had a short speaking spot at the end of the commercial.

When we were finished filming that day some of the film crew were sitting around hashing over the day and I noticed a few of them were smoking cigars and two guys were smoking pipes. This just gets better I thought. I sat down with my pipe and joined them; these people were a trip to talk to as all they wanted to talk about was different projects they had been on and different movies and television shows. This was unlike anything I had ever done. Two days later we finished filming in Castaic, loaded up the trailer and took off for Norman, Oklahoma. We were on a tight schedule so we teamed it out there. I didn't have the time on that gig but soon after that I was starting to do more film work all over the country. Sometimes we would take a break for a day during a shoot and that gave me the time to seek out tobacconist shops wherever I happened to be. On every shoot I was on there would always be someone from the immediate area that could tell me where they were.

Later that spring we did a gig that was bigger than most as it was for the F-250 and F-350 brochure for the dealers in 2005. We used the Ambassador Motel in Amarillo TX. as our base of operations for that shoot, Peggy Day was the photographer on that gig. We spent two days taking shots all over Amarillo's historic sites as well as tourist spots such as The Big Texan Steak House. The one that you get a 72 ounce steak free if you could eat all of it. Years later I worked with this other driver that wanted to try it out. On our way through Amarillo one day we all stopped there. Chet was the only one out of six of us that wanted to try. He sat at the guest of honor table reserved for the folks wanting to attempt this great feat. The rest of us sat nearby cheering him on. Chet is a real character, he sat there cool as can be and finished every scrap in front of him then just to piss them off he ordered the most expensive desert they had.

Anyway on with the shoot, after doing our thing all over town we went out to the second largest working ranch in Texas, there we filmed during a real round-up then at different picturesque locations around the ranch. We needed to rent a couple of horse trailers for a few shots and found a guy outside of town that looked to be in the wrong century. Tom was his name, horse tradin was his game. When we rented the trailers we needed another pick-up to pull an extra one out to the ranch. Tom agreed to take it out there. I rode back with him because he had a pipe in his holster attached to his belt. Besides looking like an old cowboy from 1890 and a pipe smoker I had to get to know this cat. Tom turned out to be quite a story teller; he was 75 years old and had spent his life horse tradin all over the west. He told me that he always gravitated back to Amarillo.

When my part of the shoot was done I had the rest of the afternoon to pic Tom's brain for a while. He told me about some of his more colorful adventures that took place all over the west. We had a lot in common as I had been to the areas he was talking about. Tom smoked a decent pipe that day and told me he couldn't even remember exactly when he started. He appreciated a good pipe and above average tobacco. Cigars were OK with him but he only smoked high end Cubans. He had a friend that somehow provided him with a fresh box every month. We spent a couple of hours speaking pipe speak. Tom said he used to experiment with different tobaccos until he came up with a blend that worked for him. I tried a bowl of his blend, wow it was really good. He used Nightcap by Dunhill, Plumcake by McBaren, then a rich tasting Cavendish. He told me what the ratio was, but I think he left something out as I could never duplicate it. I got close a time or two but I never hit the nail on the head with that one. Trying different variations and putting my 2 cents in some of them turned out so good that I still blend and smoke them to this day.

While sitting on a bale of hay in one of the open barns listening to Tom, Peggy Day walked up and asked me if I would be their model and precision driver the next day. Be glad to I told her, then she asked Tom to take me back into town and go to Cavenders Western Wear and get me out fitted like a cowboy, the hat and the whole bit. Tom told her not to worry he had it under control. We only had so much time before the store closed and it took 45 minutes just to get off the ranch. If Tom wanted to he could have been one hell of a dirt track driver, we flew down every shortcut he knew to get to Cavenders on the west side of town. On the way in I asked Tom what he knew about Old Tascosa west of town. There was another working ranch at this location. He knew quite a bit about it as it was part of local folklore. Legend had it that Billy the Kid and Pat Garret chased each other around out there for a while back in the day. Far out I thought. This sure beat the hell out of endlessly hauling cars to railheads and dealers in the middle of the night.

The next location was a gas. They had me drive an F-250 King Ranch model through this small creek about 40 times to get the perfect shot. I was really getting into this type of work. It sure was a lot more interesting than just hauling cars, and I was learning all kinds of new skills.

That fall I stopped into a Ford dealer and picked up an F-250 brochure and opened it up and no shit there I was covering two pages driving thru the creek with my straw cowboy hat on. How cool is that I thought. Not many truck drivers out there get a chance to do something like that.

After the Amarillo shoot, the company shipped me to Palm Springs which became my base of operations for a few months. While in the Palm Spring's the whole crew or whoever was out there working in the shop from Michigan stayed at the Ramada Inn. When getting ready for a shoot we usually worked until 5:00 in our shop then after that the time was ours.

Most of the time, everybody had a vehicle from our pool of cars at the shop so that made it easy to explore the area. I went out one evening just to look around town, during this excursion I found a Barnes and Noble Bookstore. I read all the time so this was good. Wherever I am, finding a tobacconist and a book store were the first things I looked for.

After leaving the bookstore that evening I headed further into town searching out a tobacconist shop. Address in hand I was off on a new quest. Thinking that if I was to be spending that much time in Palm Springs one must have a smoke shop to keep ones sanity intact. On the way to the tobacco shop I came upon a car dealer that sold Jaguars, Lotus, Rolls Royse, Bentley, Ferrari, and Maserati. I was in my zone I'm telling you. Every one of those cars was like the Holy Grail to me. They had this huge selection of pre-owned cars that I could wander through and dream. Walking around the lot I drew the attention of a couple of the sales people. We started talking about the cars they carried, and once they found out I was a hopeless car nut, especially for British Cars we all got along great. Instead of going out to explore the Palm Springs nightlife as the guys I worked with did. I found it more exciting to find new exotic car dealers, book stores and tobacco shops. As I was so far inland that I was starting to twitch and have other strange things going on that happens to my mind body and soul when I'm too far away from water these venues kept me in check. If I can't wonder around marinas and boat yards I'll settle for my old stand buys that I found in Palm Springs.

I spent more than a few early evenings talking to car people around the Rolls, and Jaguar dealer. I had never had the opportunity to speak with such knowledgeable people about the cars I've always been interested in. There's just something about a Rolls Royce that I just can't seem to ever get enough of. When I delivered parts to G.M. dealers there was a Cadillac dealer in Plymouth, Michigan called Don Massy Cadillac that also sold Rolls Royce motor cars. Whenever I had the extra time at that dealer I could be found out in the pre-owned lot drooling over the Rollers no matter what kind of shape they were in. For quite a few years I was a member of the Rolls Royce Owners Club. I did not own one but I was able to gather a lot of information, literature, and learn about tech stuff with the cars.

The guys at the dealership in the Palm Springs gave me a list of cigar and pipe shops in town which they recommended which gave me another quest to pursue. One Saturday I had off was spent in search of these shops. I found a few shops that I liked then some of the others I didn't so much. Not too far from the Rolls dealer was a tobacconist shop that was perfect. It had an old world tobacco shop feel to it albeit with a southern California twist. If you've ever been to southern California you know what I'm talking about.

I can't for the life of me right now remember the name of that particular shop. I do remember that it was very welcoming as the staff was extremely helpful and polite. This was not always the case with some of the shops in the area. People that came into that shop seemed like they were visiting long lost friends instead of just walking in and out.

The Tinder Box was another of my favorite shops there along with Fame Tobacco Shop. All three carried a vast selection of pipes, cigars, and fine tobacco. I didn't care for some of the shops I visited as the clientele seemed rather rich for my blood. Money can do strange things to our species.

A week after the 4th of July I got sent to San Francisco to do a week long photo shoot for Ford Magazine and to show off the new Ford Escape Hybrid to the people of said city. Thomas Hines was the photographer on the shoot and this guy couldn't stop working or rather he wouldn't till all the light was gone then he started working with available light to get even better shots.

Not being a real big production I did this gig solo. I hauled the Escape behind a Ford Dually pick-up in a one car enclosed trailer. That was fine by me as finding a place to park an 18 wheeler in the San Francisco area was all but impossible unless you wanted to dig real deep in your pocket for the required astronomical parking fees charged in the area. My company had me staying at a nice motel that had only suites with Jacuzzis. Besides that my suite over looked a small bay. Yeah life was rough doing that gig. Arriving on Sunday evening and checking in with the front desk they told me where I could leave my trailer when I was on set. My call time for the next morning was at 5:30 a.m. I wasn't that familiar with the section of town I had to be the next morning so I called a cab and took a ride. Thomas Hines studio was easy to get to so that was another plus. On the way back to the motel I asked the cab driver if he knew of any marinas in the area I was in or any close by. He drew me a map with three marinas that were not too far from the studio or the motel. I had to pinch myself as this was turning out to be a very groovy location.

I got to the studio early and rang the bell. Good morning, I'm David Senik I've got your Escape for the photo shoot. I said.

And a good morning to you, I'm Thomas Hines and you're a day early. He said actually this was a good thing as I could unload the car and park it in his garage then leave the trailer at the motel and drive the dually back and forth all week instead of having the whole rig to contend with. After getting that all taken care of I had the rest of the day off.

Comparing the cab drivers map to my San Francisco map I took off in search of boats. One of the marinas on the map was located right off of Embarcadero Drive which was a half loop type of road that you could see from the Oakland Bay Bridge if you were driving west on the bridge. I don't remember the name of the marina but it was a very kewl place. It reminded me of something right out of the movie Popeye. It had a real salty nautical look to it.

The marina might have looked a bit rickety but that was definably not so as far as the boats were concerned, in the marina they were of Bristol Fashion. Walking down the main dock I came upon a real beauty of a yacht. I noticed a gentleman working on the aft deck smoking a nice looking bent meerschaum. I told him I really admired his boat, he thanked me and invited me aboard, you sure didn't have to ask me twice.

After removing my athletic shoe's I stepped aboard. I couldn't help but notice that everywhere I looked every part of this yacht shined. The kind of magical shine that can only be achieved with loads of elbow grease and tender loving care. He introduced himself as Wayne Conner; his boat was a 55 foot Blue Water Yachts Vagabond that he affectionately named Farr Wind, this vessel reeked of being an open ocean sailing yacht. We sat in the cockpit talking about different boats in the slips that we could see from our vantage point.

Wayne told me he had grown up sailing on Lake Michigan and Lake Huron, he was from northern Wisconsin. After he left high school he joined the Navy and got stationed in the bay area and fell in love with it. After the Navy he decided to stay as he could sail all year instead of the short season we have on the Great Lakes. Wayne gave me a tour of Farr Wind, this boat was even more immaculate than I thought all the varnished surfaces had a nice deep luster. Below decks it had the aroma of English tobacco, and I noticed quite a few 100 gram tins of tobacco that had a black label with off white lettering that said London Blend hand blended by Timm from Great Briton. Besides all the cool yacht stuff to look at there were many pipe racks around the solon and navigation desk loaded with 80% meerschaum pipes. There must have been close to a hundred pipes. Back on deck the tour continued, Farr Wind was a Ketch Rig with a clipper type bow that made the lines of the boat flow like liquid. This was one of the finest yachts I'd ever laid eyes on.

We sat back down in the cockpit and talked about boats, pipes, cigars, different sailing rigs, iron sails (Engines) and whatever else popped into our feeble minds. Sitting there looking at Wayne he could have been the actor Forrest Grangers twin, although his accent wasn't British, he still had the Wisconsin, Minnesota accent going on.

It was still fairly early in the morning; Wayne said that he wanted to sail to Half Moon Bay but his sailing buddy couldn't make it. Damn I'd be glad to help you sail her over there I said. I just needed to be back tomorrow morning for work. He told me that he had a friend that ran a small plane charter service out of Half Moon and he had it all set up to catch a ride back with him late that evening and if we left right then we could make it. Sounds good to me I said. Wayne started the iron sail (engine) I untied the dock lines and we were on our way. The wind was blowing 25-30 knots out of the southwest; it would pick up significantly when we got out in the Pacific. After getting out of the marina we headed north towards the Oakland Bay Bridge. We hoisted all four sails and we started to haul ass. The Bay was just a tad rough but Farr Wind was right in her element as she was built to cross oceans. I was in the process of loading my pipe when Wayne told me to wait a minute. He turned the helm over to me and went below and came back on deck with a tin of London Blend, try this he said. He said that this was the best tasting most consistent blend he had ever found. At home he smoked a Lane bulk blend that was similar to Captain Black Royal only a bit richer as his wife declared the house her space and the boat was his space to stink up as he saw fit. I could relate to that as whenever I was around people I too smoked aromatic blends.

Passing under the Oakland Bay Bridge we could see Alcatraz Island. Every time I had traveled over that bridge I always looked down an envied the sailboats I could see. I never thought I would get the opportunity to do what I was doing at that moment in time, I felt truly blessed. Wayne was looking over a chart and looking at his GPS and suggested we make for the east side of Alcatraz so we could round the north side and sail under the Golden Gate on one tack. Thus by setting that course we would avoid some of the ship traffic.

Rounding the east side of Alcatraz and looking at it I got an eerie feeling of a dark evil forbidding place filled spirits of lost souls and hopelessness. I have seen Alcatraz many times from the bridges in the North Bay area and had always felt something like that only now it was much stronger. I have never had the urge to take a tour boat out there. I feel that some spirits are better left alone. Just the mere thought of what went on behind those walls gave me the creeps.

Our next waypoint was The Golden Gate, what a sight to behold. I had to pinch myself, from the first time I ever crossed that bridge I dreamed of what it would be like to sail under it. I also always thought of the men and women returning from war and what they must have felt when their ship passed under her. I would imagine folks got the same feeling on the Atlantic Ocean when the Statue of Liberty came into view.

And here I was about to sail under this world famous landmark on one of the finest sailing vessels I had ever seen. Besides that Skipper Wayne was quickly turning out to be one of the most interesting people I had ever met. Add to that the fact that yours truly was at the helm.

Having packed my pipe with London Blend I soon realized that the merits of it were indeed spot on. It was stout but not overwhelming without any bite. I just found a new tobacco staple to forevermore stock in my tobacco inventory. Wayne reached over and turned on the autopilot so we could kick back and enjoy the wonderful scenery. Sailing where we were, was totally different from the Great Lakes, I just started to mention this to Wayne when he said he wondered when I would say something to that effect. You just hold on, wait till we get into open water, we'll sail out of the bay for ten or so miles then head south so we can cruise into Half Moon without too much fuss.

That's just what we did, while passing under the bridge I started to feel the might of the ocean thru the helm, wow what an exhilarating sensation holding onto the wheel and feeling that kind of enormous power at my fingertips. It seemed as if Farr Wind was chomping at the bit wanting to raise her bow and go to the far reaches of the globe. To this day whenever I close my I eyes and think of the way I could feel every bit of rigging and all the sail we had up pulling on the lines and the bigger swells we were now in calms my nerves every time. What a day, what an adventure, this is what life is really about. I told Wayne the only thing that would make this day any more perfect is if Farr Wind was mine and he had a feather up his ass we'd both be tickled. We got a good laugh out of that. When we were done cracking up Wayne said hold on David it's going to get much better about a mile after we clear land you'll really feel the wonderment of the Pacific.

He was right of course, once we got further out the swells became much larger, Farr Wind was in her element as were Wayne and I. As we ventured further out the wind changed a bit coming more directly out of the west. Luckily for us Farr Wind was a dry boat, meaning that you didn't get any spray from the bow into the cockpit. Turning the helm back over to Wayne I made my way to the bow and stood out there on the bow pulpit which extended three feet or so out from the deck. Standing out there looking down into the water I felt like Leonardo Decapreo when he stood on the bow of the Titanic. Coming back into the cockpit Wayne asked me what I would do if I was sailing solo. I explained to my skipper that from an early age I've been afflicted with bend the masts, rail in the water disease. He started to crack up telling me he was also inflicted with said disease and that the only known cure was to do it, but after doing such a thing the addiction became much worse.

Let's give this filly her head and sail said the skipper. Adjusting the sails and changing course a wee bit she put her port side rail in the water and we were doing some serious sailing.

Turning south/southeast we settled in for an exciting run into Half Moon. Wayne favored a certain shipwright that did all the difficult work on Farr Wind so arriving at the marina a few hours later and finding an open slip we made fast all dock lines and after talking to Jesse the shipwright we went to the on-site restaurant where we met up with Sid (Sidney, the pilot) to have dinner before we flew back. Walking into the place we spotted Sid. He was a pipe and cigar smoker also; we couldn't smoke inside so we opted for a table outside overlooking the marina. Sitting there enjoying a beverage and a smoke I asked my two compadres if lobster and filet sounded good. They agreed that would be the right meal at the right time. Our waitress had a touch of attitude coming outside to wait on us as the wind was blowing her hair. Not wanting to spoil a fantastic day putting up with her I excused myself and found the manager and slipped him 20 bucks and requested a new waitress. While standing there another waitress came out, he asked her if she could wait on us, sure no problem she said. Right off I could tell she had a great personality and was much more cheerful than the first one. The manager went to do something and I told her that we would like not the surf and turf on the menu but the biggest lobsters and filets for each of us and to keep the libations coming, then to be sure her attitude stayed pleasant I gave her a fifty dollar bill and told her to give the check to me. (I love expense accounts)That did the trick as she turned out to be quite a hoot.

After dinner we went to a small airfield and boarded Sid's plane. Man, what a plane it was. Sid's pride and joy was a twin engine Beechcraft, it was immaculate. They told me to take a seat in the copilot's seat as they wanted to show me something on the way back to the east side of the bay. It had turned dark by this time.

We took off and it wasn't long before we were flying over the Golden Gate. Holy shit, what a view of the bridge. It's one thing to see the bridge from aerial views on television and quite another seeing it as I was right then.

Landing in a small airfield about ten miles from the marina we jumped in Sid's mid 80's vintage XJ6 (Jaguar) and made a plan. We all got along like we had known each other for years. Wayne didn't think it would take longer than a day to get the work done on Farr Wind and could we all do an all-nighter and bring her back. Sid said we should play it by ear. That was agreed upon then we exchanged phone numbers. I went back to the motel to catch a few hours' sleep before I went to the studio.

I arrived at the studio at 5:10 a.m. there was a pay parking lot a block from the studio where I could park the dually for 40 dollars a day, I paid for the rest of the week, went back to the studio where I met the rest of the crew. There was Daniel, Thomas's production assistant and right hand man, Maggie was a college student home for the summer she drove the support vehicle that carried extra cameras, computers, radios, and snacks and drinks and such, then Greg the guy from Ford Magazine, and John the guy that would write the article.

I could tell Thomas wasn't happy about something, asking him what was bothering him he told me he had talked to my boss in Palm Springs and that they didn't want him taking the Escape on the road. He said that really threw a monkey wrench into the whole shoot as the whole idea behind this shoot was to get the car out and about so that, number one the public could see it and number two that he wanted to shoot all over town, then he said that my boss told him there was no plate for the vehicle. I gave it some thought then I asked Greg if he would mind if we took it out as he was from Ford.

He said everything was up to me as I was the one prepping, driving, and taking care of the car. What about a plate Daniel asked me. Screw the plate I said that's just a mere technicality; let's get this show on the road. I had put what we called a film plate in the cargo area along with all the other stuff we would need to keep the Escape detailed.

The sun was just barely coming up when we headed to Lombard Avenue that's the famous street you see in films and television that corkscrews down a small hill and is lined with flowers and upscale houses. Thomas explained to me what kind of shot he wanted to get; he also wanted to get as many passes down the street as we could before all the tourists started showing up. They wanted some action shots with a little body role, oh boy, this is gonna be fun I thought.

Once I got to the bottom of the hill I had to go around a large city block dodging tourists and trolley cars, down I'd go again each time Thomas would reposition himself to get a different type of shot. I went down that street so many times I lost track. They kept insisting on more body roll so I gave them what they wanted. This Hybrid had a lot of pep to it. After rounding the third turn with more speed than I needed the car went up on two wheels and squealed the tires big time, they must have got the right shot. Getting back on top of the hill they all looked at me as if I had gone completely crazy. Thomas looked at me smiling saying that they sent the right guy for this shoot.

Next we went to a few historic places where we got some other good shots. We took a lunch break at a nice street side café close to the heart of the city. With a little extra time I called Wayne and asked him if he knew of any pipe shops close to where I was. He directed me to a shop just around the corner. Daniel told me that we wouldn't be taking off for another 45 minutes. Following Wayne's directions I found a nice shop that carried a vast selection of pipes along with the usual accouterments of bulk and tinned tobacco besides a better than average selection pipe accessories, as soon as I walked in the door I got that old fashioned tobacco shop feel. Their humidor was of a fairly good size with a nice selection of maduro cigars. The staff was pleasant and helpful. That day they were having a pipe sale, 40% off of the pipes in their bigger display case. They carried London Blend so I picked up a couple tins of that and picked out a nice Freehand, to this day I still can't figure out who the manufacturer is as the nomenclature wasn't stamped on the pipe very well. I'm really not all that hung up on name brands except older Ben Wades, as long as they smoke well I'm happy. For the life of me I can't remember the name of that shop. Being afflicted with CRS disease (can't remember shit) this doesn't surprise me. It sure was a nice shop though.

After lunch our little caravan went over to Treasure Island to film at a park on the water's edge. I had always wondered about this place as it is towards the western half of the Oakland Bay Bridge and the bridge goes right over it. Daniel informed me that the Island used to be all navy but not too long ago the city had purchased part of it and turned that section into a nice park. After detailing the picture car I had some time to myself so I grabbed my new pipe and sat at a table on the water's edge to try it out. I had a great view of the ships coming and going under the bridge. My new pipe turned out to be a fine smoker, much better than I expected. I was really starting to get hooked on London Blend, for a full bodied tobacco it was somewhat mild at the same time. I know that sounds a bit unusual but it's kind of hard to explain, you'd have to try it. To this day I never have been able to distinguish all the different notes in any one blend such as the testers in Pipes and Tobacco Magazine do. They must have particularly sensitive taste buds. I still try to pick out the different notes in blends but what I usually end up with is a simple do I like it or not. To read some of the tobacco reviews you would think they were describing a fine meal. It doesn't surprise in the least that I'm missing the boat on the taste bud thing as I'm sure there are plenty of pipe smokers out there that feel the same way.

After filming that day I met Wayne at the pay parking lot where I jumped in his car then headed to one of his favorite eateries up on a hill. San Francisco is a unique city as you have ever seen the up and down roads on film. Being there and driving or riding around is a gas. As we twisted and turned up one hill then down another then up a winding street to the restaurant after parking I got out of the car and turned around to take a look at the surrounding area I could see The Golden Gate and the Oakland Bay Bridge. It was getting darker out and the lights on the bridges were a sight to behold. We picked a table outside so we could smoke, sitting there looking at the city and bridges was a bit surreal. I kept taking pictures with high speed film until I ran out of it. I didn't know where we would be shooting the next day as I don't think Thomas had even decided yet. Wayne told me to just give him a call wherever I was and he would direct me to a pipe shop as there were many scattered around the city.

I think I took as many if not more pictures as Thomas did that week. I kept buying more film until Thomas gave me a couple dozen rolls of 35 millimeter film as he had switched over to digital for his studio.

The next morning we shot at Fisherman's Warf and yes the clam chowder is as good as they say it is. After that we went to a park below the Golden Gate on the south side to get set up for a series of shots crossing the bridge. The crew had rented a Volkswagen convertible so they could get the right shots crossing the bridge. I was reasonably under the impression that with the top down that Thomas would take pictures from there. Nope, he wanted to sit in the trunk and shoot pictures while crossing said bridge. Damn I thought this dude is just as crazy as I am. Remember the new VW Bug has the engine in front instead of in the rear. I didn't think we'd be able to get on the bridge with him in the trunk. Before we attempted this feat we had to tie Thomas into it so he could use both hands, after strapping him in he was able to close the trunk most of the way. Off we went, it all worked out well, we made three trips across, it was a blast driving across that bridge with Thomas hanging out of that small space of a trunk taking pictures in front on the side and rear. People in other cars and trucks were getting a kick out of it too, giving us the thumbs up and honking their horns.

On the third pass we wound up on the north side and took the first exit, driving under the bridge we headed up the hill to a lookout park on top, all the while Thomas is hanging out of the bug shooting. On top of the hill we had a picturesque view of the bridge and San Francisco, since then I have recognized that vantage point in many films and television shows. The same holds true for that famous row of houses that are painted a multitude of colors and the houses are on a grade heading downhill. We took pictures in a park right across the street from there so we could get the houses in the shot.

Every day was a new adventure on that shoot; San Francisco is one of the most unique cities I've ever been to. Being able to spend a week there and going all over the place was very cool indeed.

The Escape was painted a nice metal flake light green with silver accents on the bottom, it was a good looking car. There were also Hybrid decals on each side of the rear windows. The color scheme set it off in a classy way. Wherever we went people would gather around and start asking questions about it. That made the folks from Ford magazine very happy. They were taking a lot of pictures of the people looking it over to take back to Ford, which I'm sure made them more than a little happy. Another thing that amazed me was the fact that for five days I drove that car all over the city and I never had to put gas in it. This car was fun with a capital F it was so peppy I couldn't resist stabbing the gas every chance I got. This little Hybrid crossover had more balls than a Chinese Ping Pong Ball Tournament. That's saying a lot considering every time you turned there would be another hill to climb. We spent half of a day at the Presidio. I OK'd it with Thomas and took Wayne with us that day, him being a Navy man he enjoyed himself. Before leaving town he gave me a new Meerschaum carved in the likeness of a waterman, I still have that pipe, every time I smoke it I think about the wonderful time I had in that special city. For many years I kept in touch with Wayne until his passing in 2009. I miss my pipe smoking friend;

wherever he's at I picture him with a bent Meerschaum in his mouth sailing through the heavens.

Arriving back in Palm Springs I had a day off and spent the morning looking at cars in the Rolls dealers lot, then went to a few tobacco shops and spent the rest of the day enjoying a nice cigar, my new pipes, London Blend, and a book sitting by the pool.

The next day was spent getting a few cars ready for a commercial that would be filmed at one of the major studios located in Santa Monaca, California. This was going to be a week long film shoot so we took a lot of extra parts and manpower to the set. What made this film shoot different was that it was being filmed right down the street from the courthouse used in the Back to the Future movies. If that wasn't cool enough the commercial called for them to make a snow storm in July. It was interesting walking around the lot looking at different sets, people walking around with period costumes and clothing from all walks of life around the globe.

The more involved I became with the film industry the more differently I began to watch movies and television. Like my dad, Daniel Senik I'm a real movie buff. I remember coming home from grade school while he worked nights we would watch Bill Kennedy at the Movies on channel 56. Watching that show you could be sure of one thing and that was that Bill would without fail be smoking something.

I was fortunate when filming at different locations in California I was able to visit many Tobacconist shops. I never went into one without purchasing something. More times than not they were super cool shops but once in a while I'd happen upon one that was a real dud. Even in those shops I always bought something weather I needed it or not, I appreciated them being there.

What amazed me then as now was that California is one of the most anti-tobacco states we have but the tobacconist shops are exquisite. Food for thought, eh.

My self and Burt a coworker did a large production film shoot with the new Retro Mustang that was coming out that fall. We did this gig in and around Pasadena, California. Besides being able to drive and work with the new Mustang, the photographer on that film shoot had a great-great grandfather who was Samuel Clemens (Mark Twain) being a big fan of Twain's, this was beyond cool. While talking to one of his production assistance I learned that he did mostly boat and yacht pictures for such magazines as Wooden Boat, Sail, and others. That gig was a lot of fun, the crew and I were speaking boat speak whenever we got the chance. I've been reading Wooden Boat Magazine for twenty years so talking about some of the classic yachts they worked with was extra kewl.

One day we set up in an alley where the set crew built a set that looked like a French café. The cars were positioned so the people in the café and the cars were visible. After the cars were ready I had some time before they started filming so I went in search of a pipe shop. After enquiring a few locals I was directed to a nice Tobacconist Shop two blocks from the set.

If I remember correctly it was called Rose Tobacconist. It was a fairly good sized shop, with a great selection of new and estate pipes. I've never had a problem with estate pipes as some people do. I like the fact that their already broken in and that you can get a lot of pipe for the money.

Looking over the estate pipes I spied two nice briar calabash pipes that upon closer inspection looked brand new. For quite some time I had been looking for a pipe just like the ones I was checking out. The proprietor made me a deal on both of them. Looking over their house blends they smelled unique, after picking a few blends to purchase the owner told me all the blends the house put together were concocted by the previous owner and he never changed them as they seemed perfect for his clientele who bought their blends in large quantities. He also had a long mailing list he sent tobacco to, who had visited the shop during all the Rose Bowl celebrations.

Arriving back on set there wasn't anything for me to do for a while so I kicked back and tried one of my new and old pipes and the recommended house blends. The first pipe I tried gave me that warm contented feeling you get handling and smoking one of your favorite pipes. The blend I put in my pipe first was a Virginia with some components I couldn't put my finger on but it was one of the better blends that I've ever tried. Both Calabash pipes turned out to be excellent smokers.

A week or two after that I took a new Mustang to the set of Orange County, the TV show with Peter Gallagher in it. The location was in a subdivision in Malibu Beach, the crew and all the production equipment plus the wardrobe, makeup, catering truck, and honey wagon (out houses) were all set up on the beach at a park. Just getting there was fun as I had the car on an open one car trailer behind a dually all of our other trucks and trailers were on different sets. The public had seen the car in pictures or at auto shows but this was the first time that Ford allowed it to travel on an open trailer so you can imagine the attention it got going from Palm Springs to Malibu.

I had to be on set at 5:00 in the morning. After arriving and talking to the set people I followed a director to the subdivision they were filming at where I positioned the car and detailed it for the days shooting. After that I had the whole day to myself as they wouldn't be done filming until around six that evening.

Asking around nobody could tell me where a tobacco shop was so I unhooked from the trailer and went in search of pipes. Before I found a tobacconist I came upon a surf shop, I just had to stop and see what was new and improved on the surf scene. Like tobacconist shops I love to visit surf shops, dive shops, and marina stores. The beach was right out the back door and a short walk across the beach. I hadn't planned on it but when I got into the store they had boards to rent, so after purchasing some surf trunks and wax I rented a board and hit the surf. The waves were not real big that day but big enough to get a decent ride.

Paddling out I was thinking that maybe I was a little off my rocker as here I was at 50 years old going out to catch some waves. Rethinking those thoughts, this was too much fun not to do it. Then I thought why act your age, you're as young as you feel and I felt like surfing. After getting out to where you could catch the waves there were a few other guys my age out there too. Waiting for the right set to come in we all introduced ourselves, one of the guys was 62 so I felt young or should I say younger.

It took me a few attempts but I finally got up on a nice wave and started getting my groove back. All of us stayed out in the surf for a couple hours then went in to the beach. The older guys name was Sam Young (yes his real name) after rinsing of the salt water and changing I took Sam back to the set location so he could see how they made TV shows and to grab a nice meal from the catering truck. As far as they were concerned Sam was working with me. We finished eating then Sam reached in his pocket and pulled out a nice looking briar freehand. I slapped my knee and said, well I'll be damned, I knew there was something about you that was off kilter. Sam gave me a quizzical look then I grabbed one of my pipes from the cab then he got it. We sat there looking out at the ocean and talked about pipes. Sam was a retired aerospace engineer and had been smoking a pipe for over 40 years. Sam told me that just about all of his brilliant ideas came to him while he smoked his pipe. I told him I was looking for a smoke shop when I came across the surf shop, and at that time and moment the surf shop trumped the smoke shop search. Smoking our pipes in silence for a few minutes we both agreed that what happened with me seeing the surf shop had to be some type of divine intervention.

He said he could take me to his tobacconist if I still wanted to go if I had time as it was only a few miles away. Let's go I said, we got into his car which was unique in its own right as it was a maroon colored Avanti in pristine condition with a surfboard rack on top. In my book this qualified as some knarly cool shit. In Sothern California this was not that uncommon of a site, but anywhere else in the country it would be. You have to understand that was everyday stuff there, it is definitely not the case when it comes to the rest of the world; I mean that in a good and positive way.

I asked him what his family and friends thought of him being a 62 year old pipe smoking surfer. My wife's cool with it and as far as anyone else is concerned he didn't give a fat rats ass what they thought. This I thought was a fine outlook to have indeed.

We arrived at Surfside Smokes, entering I was taken back as the shop had a nautical, beachside décor to it, unlike any shop I had ever been in. Sam knew the owner quite well as he had been buying his supplies there for years. After busting balls with Sam and the owner for a bit, smoking out on the patio he told me whatever I bought would be 30% off. Well now, I must purchase something unique and memorable to keep this memory fresh. I picked out some custom pipe tampers and a large bent Peterson. At least one of the tampers would forever rest upon my person in one of my pockets wherever I went to remind me of that day and that you're never too old to enjoy the things that float yer boat.

After loading the car that day I went to Pasadena and got a room for the night at the Holiday Inn. I had to deliver the car to the California Speedway the next morning in Fontana, California for a hot rod custom car show they were having that weekend. After unloading the car in the infield at the Ford tent I was to free scope out the show. I turned the car over to Ford and Event Solutions; they would be the ones to take over the car as they were scheduled to take it to different events around the country.

Returning to Palm Springs I dropped my trailer at our yard then re-checked into the Ramada Inn where we all stayed when in town and had the rest of the weekend off. This was rather unique as one day I was sitting on a surfboard in the Pacific Ocean the next I was in the desert, one extreme to another.

I was going to go for a swim in the pool but it was packed with party revelers having a grand time so I put that off till evening and went to the Rolls dealer to see what was new on the lot and to shoot the breeze with some of the sales people I had gotten to know.

While I was looking over a nice Jaguar XJS that had come onto the pre-owned lot this fine looking semi came onto the rear driveway. Well now what do we have here I thought. This might be interesting; I knew he had to be delivering high end cars as this was an enclosed trailer, besides what else could he be unloading there.

The truck and trailer were all black with a wide silver stripe down each side and all the chrome and aluminum were highly polished. I was just going to stand back and watch but then the driver let the lift gate down and I could see inside the trailer. Holy shit, he had two brand new Rolls Royse Phantoms in there. To me this was one of the finest motor cars ever built. These were the new style that looks very commanding. This model was one of the stateliest vehicles ever produced, all hand made in England with leather interior and a paint job that had a luster that only Rolls Royce could achieve. I walked up and started talking to the driver. His name was Richard LaPree he told me to call him Dickey that everybody did. Of course I didn't know it at the time but Dickey and I would become close friends. Knowing my way around an enclosed trailer I helped him unload two Rolls Royce's and a Bentley Arnage. I told Dickey I could get into this as he let me position the cars in the lot. I've always been under the assumption that if you appreciate whatever you drive, you never just park it, you POSITION it. After the cars were unloaded and we closed up the trailer I asked him if he had time for dinner, it was on me if I could pick his brain for a bit. Sure he said so after making sure it was OK to leave his rig there for a while I took him back to the Ramada for dinner as they had an excellent restaurant and lounge.

During dinner I asked him what all his company did, I knew they hauled exotic cars but that was about all. Dickey informed me not only did they transport high end autos, they also did commercials, videos, car shows such as Pebble Beach Concurs and POV's (personally owned vehicles) for people in the spotlight such as actors, actresses, sports figures, singers, and the like. This was starting to sound more interesting than what I was currently doing. Their equipment was nice, all newer Kenworth trucks and trailers to match.

We sat and talked for quite a spell after dinner. Dickey without too much arm twisting persuaded me to jump ship and go to work for Pilot Transport out of Brighton, Michigan. That's what I did, I was getting the itch to get back out there and see the country again as there had been many changes around the U.S. since I had last drove all 49 states and Canada. (Yes I had been to Alaska in a semi)

Getting back to Michigan I gave my notice and hired on with them. They assigned me to an older Kenworth that had been neglected by the previous driver. The aluminum wheels and everything else on the truck were Dull with a capital D, this just won't do I thought, like anything else I've ever driven I looked at it with a knowing eye that I could see this rig had possibilities. I asked dispatch if they could send me to either southern California or Phoenix so I could stop into one of my two favorite polish shops. My boss and head dispatcher Joe Parks said he wanted to send me to the east coast then west after that. I told him that if I had to drive something that far that didn't shine like a new nickel that it could cause irreversible harm to my psyche and that was also detrimental to my health and overall wellbeing and health. Being the great guy that Joe is he just shook his head and gave me paperwork for a load going to the California Speedway.

Three and a half days later I unloaded at the speedway then with the rest of day off and before I had to pick the cars back up I went to Three Sisters Truck Wash and Polish shop in Hesperia, California. Three Sisters is a bit spendy but they do one hell of a job. By the following evening I had the rig in fine shape it certainly didn't look like the same rig. This I could live with, I just needed some chrome accessories any driver worth his salt would have adorning his pride and joy. Your truck is not only your workspace it's also your home, so the more you take care of it the more it will take care of you. One must take pride in their ride no matter what it may be. I swear that after all the waxing and polishing was done and I started her up I heard her breathe a sigh relief and say thank you. Maybe that was all in my head but I think not.

After loading the cars at the speedway I had room for one more so they brought me back to our warehouse in Phoenix to pick up a Ferrari going to a dealer in Orchard Lake, Michigan. While there I pulled into Danny's Big Rig Resort on 67th Ave. to get the oil and all filters changed, most people called this place Danny's Diesel. This place is unique in the fact that they have six bays for oil changes, mechanical work, and tires, then next four bays for truck washes. They also have nice showers, a café, a big TV room, and a well-stocked chrome shop. Walking out the back door there are picnic tables and even a small stream with gold fish, considering where it's at, it's a relaxing place to unwind from the hustle and bustle of the road, especially if you just came out of Los Angeles. Getting the truck outfitted with the proper chrome in all the right places I was ready to do some serious trucking and that's just what I did. Besides transporting high end cars we also hauled test and development cars for all the automotive manufacturers. These autos would be loaded with computers and gages that gathered info that was used to develop new models. I had to sign confidentiality agreements as I often went into proving grounds all over the country where I could see prototypes and vehicles the rest of the world would never see. Many times I loaded cars I was requested to load under the cover of darkness, sometimes inside a building. Doing these sight sensitive moves was unique. We were told to never disclose where we were taking our load and to never tell anyone what was inside the trailer. Entering most facilities I had to hand over any cameras and phones if there was a camera in it. Being a car nut this type of work was the cats' ass.

During this time I stayed busy transporting Ferraris and Maserati's from the Port of Newark, New Jersey to the west coast. Hollywood. California. Thousand Oaks, California and Scottsdale, Arizona, were the basic destinations for these cars. Then the new Bentley GT's came out which we loaded out of Charleston, South Carolina these cars were nice. I hadn't been on the east coast for quite a few years. It was crowded the last time I was out there and much more so this time around.

One of the main destinations for these autos was North Jersey, Manhattan, and Greenwich, Connecticut. I had already taken a few loads up to Manhattan, on my first run up to Manhattan heading up I-95 in North Carolina I started seeing signs for J.R.'s Tobacco about a hundred and fifty miles before I got there. Driving by the exit I tried to figure out if I could park my rig there or close by so I could go into the smoke shop. This J.R.'s was a lot different than the one in Michigan as it was much bigger and according to the billboards carried all kinds of stuff. Their parking lot didn't look like it was semi friendly; I did see some RV's but no room for trucks. Just south of the building about three hundred yards was an abandoned gas station of some sort I had seen a truck in but it looked like a tight fit; I would have to take up the whole shoulder and then some if I wanted to park there.

On one of these New York runs I timed it so that I could pull into J.R.'s when they opened thinking I had a better chance of parking. Coming up to the Selma, North Carolina exit I slowed down to see if I could park at the gas station. I didn't want to get off the exit unless there was room for me to park. I was in luck that day as there wasn't anyone parked in the station. It was a tricky maneuver but I got my rig positioned and headed for the door.

I really didn't know what to expect upon entering, this place was much bigger than what I thought. They sold a little bit of everything besides a lot of books and tobacco. My kind of joint for sure. They also had large models of sailing ships, pleasure cruisers and such. OK then I thought, stopping here could become habit forming for someone like myself.

Giving things the once over I made my way to the humidor. This wasn't just any humidor, it was located in the middle of the store and I would guess was around 100 feet by 50 feet. Wow, I'd never been to such a big cigar store, it was rather mesmerizing, there were boxes of cigars stacked everywhere. Wanting all this to soak in I took my sweat assed time wandering through it, besides I wasn't going to deliver in the Apple until the following morning. For me to be in a place like this I knew I'd be in deep shit and a lot lighter in the money department if I didn't watch myself.

They had every type of pipe and cigar you could think of and then some. I spotted a nice and fine looking Toro Maduro that looked tasty under the glass counter and bought it to smoke as I meandered through the store. There were several nice plush leather arm chairs around that one could sit and enjoy a smoke. Settling into on, lighting my cigar I just sat and tried to take in the enormity of my surroundings. The inside of the store gave you an old time feel; it has a wooden floor which creaks when you walk across the place. It reminded me of a store in Howell called Swans Store, the owner Doug Swan was a longtime friend of my fathers that I had worked for when I was quite young. The thing that made Swans special was the creaky wooden floors. The store carried everything clothing and boot wise for the working man, everything in that store is union made. People from all around would come there to shop.

Anyway, back to J.R.'s, as I sat smoking enjoying the vastness of the place I found a catalogue that I could look thru. Like J.R.'s in Michigan, the first time I went in there was overwhelming. I picked out a box of J.R.'s Ultimate's and a 10 cigar box of Arturo Fuente Cannons then made my way over to the pipe section. J.R.'s have a huge selection of tinned pipe tobacco offered at substantially lower prices than anyplace I've ever found. Not knowing when I'd have another chance to come in here I stocked up on quite a few tins. I too at times buy a tin of tobacco purely by the picture or graphics on it.

I spent about two hours in there and a few hundred bucks that maybe I shouldn't have, but maybe being the operative word here I soon talked myself into the mindset that I was being a wise shopper. Yes, there might be a little truth to the belief that pipe and cigar smokers thought pattern is a bit different from the masses. As I've mentioned before, normal scares me. After turning this all over in my feeble mind I was quite proud of myself and of my wise purchases.

Making my way up the coast I was halfway up the New Jersey Turnpike when I got a call from the office telling me I was scheduled to load Ferraris out of the Port of Newark the next day. I had planned on spending the night in the Vince Lombardi Service Plaza on the New Jersey turn pike, but I wanted to get back to Jersey as soon as I could the next day, load the trailer and get the hell out of Dodge as it would be Friday and getting out would be a bitch in the late afternoon. Besides I thought it would be damn near impossible to get across the George Washington Bridge at 5:00 p.m. let alone make it down the 150 blocks I needed to go down to Broadway. What the heck I thought maybe it would turn into an adventure. I kept going, crossing the bridge without any trouble then headed down Broadway. That turned out to be just as hectic as I thought. Some drivers hate that type of traffic, being in a sea of cabs and what have you. I viewed it as a challenge, sure the antics of the cabbies and others were unpredictable but that to me was the allure.

Traveling down Broadway in the light of early evening I kept a weather eye out for the smoke shop I had stopped at years before. Not too many blocks from where I needed to turn right I spotted it. Far out I thought, if I can park (position) my rig just north of the dealer I could walk or take a cab to it.

The dealer is located in south Manhattan, you turn on 37th heading west for two blocks then hang a left and a block before the dealer is a bridge that semis park on. Luckily there was a spot open. I called some of our other drivers that had delivered there to see if they knew of any New York Delis close by, nobody did so after checking on my cars in the trailer I was locking up when a NYPD cop pocked his head in the door to look at the cars. We started talking and I invited him in the trailer to take a better look. He thought that was cool, I asked him if he knew of the smoke shop up the road and sure he knew of it and it was still open. Keith was the cops name; he asked if I would like a ride up there. Hell yeah I said, on the way I learned he liked cigars. I asked him if he knew of a good deli in the area, he laughed and said one of the best in the city was also somewhat close by but it was a bit spendy. No problem I said, how bout dinner I asked him it's on me I appreciate the ride. Great he said but my break isn't for another couple hours. That works just fine I said. We went up Broadway past the shop where Keith made a u turn, parked in front of the place on the road and flipped his blooper lights on saying he'd go in with me and give me a ride back. Now I ask you, how cool is that, being escorted to a smoke shop by one of New York's Finest!

We went in and low and behold the same dude that waited on me years before was still there. He actually recognized me after a minute. After shaking hands with him I let him tell Keith about the time I blocked most of the southbound lanes the day I went into his shop. I found a nice Savaneli Strait Grain estate pipe for a decent price; I picked up a can of briar pipe wipe, some pipe cleaners, and a few smoker candles. They were having a half-price sale on Macanudo Cigars that looked tasty, I noticed Keith looking at a box of Macanudo Diplomat Maduro's, I like a longer cigar so I spotted some Lord Nelson Churchill's. They all were good smokes and for half off how could I with somewhat of a sane mind pass up that kind of deal.

Picking up two boxes of the Diplomats and two boxes Churchill's along with their more popular house blends I was done. Getting back into Keith's squad car I pulled the Diplomats out of the bag and gave them to Keith thanking him for the job he did. I know I could never do it but I had great respect for cops. How they keep a good attitude is beyond me, especially when you consider some of the people they deal with on a daily basis. He wouldn't take them at first but I talked him into it. Dropping me off at my truck he said I'll see you in a couple hours.

Walking back into my sleeper I grabbed one of my older better pipes then put together a couple bags of tobacco I figured a Maduro smoker would like. Keith didn't know it yet but I was going to turn him into a pipe smoker.

Sitting in the driver's seat catching up on paper work Keith pulled in front of the truck, got out and informed me that he didn't have to work overtime that night so if 10:00 wouldn't be too late we could eat then and would I mind if some of his squad joined us. Of course not I said, looking forward to it.

Two and a half hours later he came back in an unmarked car with three of his squad members. We went to a deli two blocks away. This place was in between two bigger stores, it had a dozen tables and a deli counter the likes of which I'd never seen before. Any type of meat or cheese you could think of was there. All of us ordered and sat down, somehow the conversation shifted to 9/11, these guys were there, close by the buildings when they came down. Hearing the story's first hand from people that were actually on site that day was unforgettable. The hell they went through that day and the days after was something to hear. We sat and talked for a good two hours.

Before they took me back to my rig Keith and I exchanged phone numbers and I gave him the pipe and tobacco I had picked out, telling him to give it a try and to just call me and I'd be glad to walk him through the process of smoking a pipe. Two days later I got a call from him telling me that he got with an older detective that smoked a pipe and so far he was enjoying it even more so than cigars. Another convert, we need all of them we can get.

After unloading in New York, I made good time to Newark and loaded six Ferraris, one for Jackson, Mississippi, one for

Houston, Texas, one for Scottsdale, Arizona and the remaining three to Hollywood, California. Out of Newark I took I-78 to I-81 to I-75 to I-59, into I-20 then across I-20 into Jackson, Mississippi. After not being fulltime over the road for the past 10 years it was interesting and sad at the same time to see all the changes that had taken place around the country. Where there used to be character in the different truck stops and exits, now it seemed that no matter what exit I went by in whatever state I was in it was all the same. They're like pods of the same thing every exit. This I didn't care for, as they seemed to suck the personality out of towns, making them carbon copies of each pod. You could pick up one pod in any state and drop it in another and nobody would know the difference. That's what used to be one of the best parts of traveling around the country. Every state, town, or city had its own aura to it. I was finding out in a hurry this wasn't the case anymore. To this day thinking about it saddens me.

What happened to this great country made up of a vast assortment of people and places? I was starting to crave the diners of old. That old saying of, go to the restaurants where the trucks park because they must have good food is a myth. The reason nine times out of ten was that we were able to park there. It really didn't have anything to do with the food, although there were many cafés and diners across the states that did have excellent chow.

Around Huntsville, Alabama, I started seeing all manner of vehicles packed inside and out with what looked like all the belongings of the folks in vehicles. It reminded me of the old pictures I had seen of the people leaving the dust bowl with everything they could carry with them. This looked the same, the only thing different was the modern forms of transportation they were traveling in. Since I left Newark I had been listening to books on cd, that being one of my favorite forms of entertainment on the road. I hadn't even listened to the news in days. Switching off my book I turned on the CB and asked what was up with the mass exodus from the south, Katrina was all someone said. Who or what is Katrina I asked, big assed hurricane another driver answered back. Well shit, I better turn on the news I thought. Tuning to the national weather channel on my satellite radio I found out that a storm, the likes of which hasn't been seen in decades was on its way to wreak havoc and destruction on the Gulf Coast. The further I went the more families I observed fleeing the Big Easy area. As I mentioned earlier in the book I spent some time in that neck of the woods. Being familiar with most of the Redneck Riviera I was concerned as that part of the country is extremely low lying land.

I was making great time and made it to my stop in Jackson then went to Vicksburg, Mississippi. Thinking I'd get a decent meal take a shower and spend the night there as this was one of the nicer truck stops in that area. I'm glad I got there early; the place was packed with RV's and all manner of vehicles setting up camp for the night.

After fueling and checking all the fluids in my truck I went in to get a shower before eating. Inside by the fuel desk was mass confusion, all the people were buying as much gas and diesel as there rides would hold. Standing in line in front of me was a family of four wanting to get showers; after the father heard the price of ten bucks a pop I could see him and his wife having a conversation with their eyes that said, that was too much. I had seven showers on my fuel card as every time I put 50 gallons in my truck I got a credit for a shower. I let them use my truck stop card to get there showers.

Walking into the restaurant I sat by a window so I could observe the comings and goings in the lot, always good entertainment you see some wacky things. I was looking at all the loaded down vehicles remembering when I lived in Oregon there was a forest fire on the next ridge over from where I lived. The forest service came by and told me to get ready to evacuate if the wind shifted. So I knew something about what these folks were going through.

Katrina was still two and a half days away, I figured being as far south as I was I'd better get as far west as possible. That being said I hit the road early next morning, staying with it all day and into the night I figured even if the storm hit before scheduled I was far enough west not to worry about it. I kept seeing caravan after caravan of Fema trucks heading towards the storm area. My friend Dickey was up on I-40 running a couple hundred miles in front of me. He was seeing the same thing up there.

The rest of the run went well; I enjoyed my new pipes and tobacco cruising across the desert. With some of the new tobacco I had to stop smoking some of it on account of it relaxed me too much, getting sleepy behind the wheel was not an option.

Having delivered my load I met up with Dickey in Carson, California where our drivers usually stayed at the Hampton Inn. Dickey had been there for a day already and scoped out a rib joint, so after checking in we went over there. We sat in the rib shack watching the devastation of Katrina on the tube. As you know what happened I won't go into it. Looking at the map of the wide area that was hit I said, sonofabitch that hurricane hit St. James Parish. The folks at the next table asked what was so great about that, I should be concerned about New Orleans instead of some po dunk spit of a town. Up yours pal I said, that's the only place in this whole world that makes Perique pipe tobacco. I was seriously worried, what if we couldn't get Perique in our favorite blends. This storm could be much worse than anybody could speculate.

We went back over to the Inn to watch more news coverage. My phone rang it was the office asking me if I was up for a two week commercial gig in Vancouver British Columbia for Acura. It loaded the day after next, so that gave me a day to get my laundry done and stock up on supplies.

Next morning we went to the mall across from the Inn and low and behold there was a tobacconist shop called The Corona in the mall, they had a nice selection of cigars and pipe tobacco the pipes were nice also. I had spent so much on pipes that trip that I figured I'd better enjoy the ones I had before accumulating more.

I went to Sun Valley, California to load which took the better part of the day as we loaded extra dashboards, seats, wheels and tires and other odds and ends, besides all the tools the car prep guys doing the shoot needed, besides the six cars in the trailer.

Leaving there I felt like truckin so I got over the Grapevine then through Emerald Valley, past Sacramento to where the I-5 meets the 505 to a truck stop that used to be called Pantyhose Junction because the waitresses all wore short skirts and pantyhose. Back in the day in the restaurant you got your thermos filled for free if you had a Pantyhose Junction sticker on it. I pulled off the ramp not really knowing what to expect. In my feeble mind I hoped that the old place would still be there. It wasn't, in its place was a Pilot Truck Stop with a fast food joint inside. My how things change.

It was nice traveling up I-5 not having been there in many years. A couple of my old favorite stops were still there but most weren't. Climbing the Sisque Mountain between California and Oregon I bailed off the north side and proceeded up into my old stomping grounds. I was heartbroken to see that most of the old family owned saw mills had closed down. Most of the towns I went thru were almost unrecognizable compared to what they once were. It was still enjoyable seeing that big country again. Washington State was still basically the same till I got to the Tacoma area in which it had grown by leaps and bounds.

Because of the rag head psychopath dipshits crashing our planes into our buildings, crossing into Canada was a pain in the ass. I pulled into the holding lot at the border and made contact with the broker to get the extra documentation to enter the Maple Leaf Country. After that I went into another building to get my papers signed, there I was told I had to unload the whole trailer so these asshole border dudes could check the vin numbers on the cars to make sure they were the ones listed on the paperwork. Now it took me and four other guys that knew what they were doing six and a half hours to get everything loaded on my trailer. I was of pissed off. Four border cops followed me to the truck I opened the side door so they could see that getting everything out would be a challenge. They took a look inside and wanted to know how long it would take to unload it and If all the vins matched I could reload. I was as nice as I could be to them. After explaining that the load was going to a film shoot for Acura and that with everything out of the trailer it would not only take many hours, I would be taking up a huge amount of space in the lot.

Then they came up with the brilliant idea that they would get in the trailer, crawl around on both decks and call out the VIN numbers to an officer on the ground outside. I explained to them that these cars were painted with a special rubber paint that scratched easily. Then I asked them if they could remove all the hardware on their belts including their guns. Oh no, we can't do that I was told. OK how about if I get in there and call the vins out to you guys. I explained to them that maneuvering around in there was dangerous and that I didn't want any of them to get hurt falling thru a deck breaking a leg or arm. One of them said I might have the vins memorized. I informed them that I hauled so many cars sometimes I couldn't even remember what I had in there let alone memorize the vins for six cars. This went over well with all but one of the gun hoe dudes. He was told to leave by another officer. Then I grabbed a small mag lite climbed into the trailer and proceeded to call out the numbers.

I kept a thermometer on the right side in the middle of the trailer which read 120 degrees in there. Whenever I got in the trailer to check on my load, I always without fail wear a pair of coveralls that were made so as not to scratch the cars. After sweating off five pounds, everything checked out and I was on my way.

The plan was to meet up with the car prep crew and some of the artists and directors at an airfield south of town. Of course as you've probably guessed I was the only one that drove there. Once there I had to unload a car so the artists could sketch and take numerous pictures so they could begin their work. After that

I secured the truck and hopped in a rental SUV the car prep guys and I would use to get around for the next two weeks.

Throwing my bag into the support vehicle we were off to the motel, and what a motel it was. Everyone on the shoot was booked into the Weston Motel in downtown Vancouver. We checked in and were to meet the whole crew in one of the conference rooms to go over that week's itinerary. Roberto was the head guy for B.A.D. the company doing the prep work besides me. I knew what I was doing on a film shoot so they were happy to have me there instead of a green horn.

Sitting down next to Roberto he handed me an envelope, I looked inside and there was a thick stack of one hundred dollar bills. I asked what this was for, Roberto said that it was perdium for me from his company because I knew my stuff and would be helping them. There was twelve hundred bucks in there. This I could get used to. I mean how cool was that and being able to stay at such a swanky motel for two weeks and have extra cash in me pocket. Life was good!

During the meeting I found out that most of the film crew was from France. Others from southern California and still others from all over the globe. The next day we were to film just below a ski resort up one of the surrounding mountains. We were going to work with a helicopter taking aerial shots. Cool I thought, after that the rest of the day was all mine. I went back to my room, grabbed a pipe and went in search of a pipe shop.

Leaving the lobby I picked up a city guide and map so I could familiarize myself with where I was and where my truck was. Always a good thing to do in a strange place. I went across the street to a Starbucks, got a cup of coffee and sat outside smoking my pipe scoping out the maps. Having gotten a grip on my location I went back inside to ask where I could find a smoke shop. Things are different in British Columbia as opposed to in the states. Following the directions I was given I walked a block and a half and stood in front of an establishment called WEEDS. As in the heathen devil weed Marijuana, damn I thought, sure is different here than down below in the 48's. Hmm I better go in and investigate this place. Entering I was hit by a strong odor of incense, looking around they had anything you could ever possibly think of to assist you in your quest for higher personal elevation. Well now what a unique establishment I thought. Some of the merchandise I knew what it did but there was quite a bit I had no earthly clue. Not being one that took part in that type of weed I was getting an education from the staff. In so many words they told me that if I worded what strain of weed I wanted in a certain way they could oblige me in their special product and rest assured they could help me on my way to higher learning of the fine art of medicinal weed therapy. I had been into head shops in the 70's but this place was way beyond those. I pulled my pipe out of my pocket and told them what I was really looking for was a more conventional type of smoke. One of the girls asked me how I wound up there instead of a tobacconist shop. I told her that I asked for directions to a smoke shop in Starbucks and they sent me here. I was informed that a smoke shop in Vancouver meant something entirely different than what I was accustomed to. No shit I thought, I must get more in tune to my new surroundings. They gave me directions to a well-known Tobacconist just a block away.

Finding my next stop I was greeted to a fine old time type smoke shop. Telling the staff what I had just done they got a laugh out of it telling me that quite a few people from the states make the same blunder. I bought a couple of their house blends and a tin of Plumcake as for some unknown reason I had a craving for it. I hung out there shooting the shit with the staff for a couple hours when it hit me hey, I'm in Canada; I can buy Cuban cigars here. They helped me pick out a few nice dark Maduro's, let me tell you, they were not cheap. I went back to the coffee shop where I cut one and had an enjoyable smoke at an outside table.

One thing that amazed me being there was all the different languages that were being spoken; I was definitely not in Kansas anymore. Another thing I found interesting was the negativity in which people spoke about America. I felt like voicing my opinion on this but decided it best if I kept my yap shut. I couldn't help but think that nobody wants America around until they need us to win a war or help them in their ass backwards country in time of need because their too damn ignorant to be prepared as we Americans are. As a proud American I held my head high and when asked didn't hesitate to tell whoever asked me that yes I was from the BADASS country, and that no you do not want to PISS us off. We band together rather quickly to meet any obstacle in our way. And that my friend has been proven time and time again.

Anyway on the fourth day the car crew and I met at the valet parking area to get our support vehicle. I walked outside with my coffee thinking I had time for a morning pipe when I noticed a well-dressed couple that looked to be in their 70's sitting on a bench right outside the motel door passing a joint back and forth waiting for their Cadillac to be brought around. The man noticed me looking at them and with a European accent asked me if I would like to partake with them. I politely declined and sat down wind from them and lit my pipe. Roberto came out, took a sniff of the air then looked over to me, I nodded my head towards the couple, and he smiled, shook his head and sat next to me. What a city!

On this gig we shot film for a day or two then moved to different locations and would have a day off. We went on a couple of float plane rides, and did some of the other tourist stuff. My favorite thing to do was to take water taxi tours of the harbor and marinas. I was surprised at the number of boats anchored all over the harbor and marinas that people lived aboard. I thought that was very cool indeed.

After finishing up in Vancouver I took the cars back to Sun Valley then I went to Carson and got a room for my day off by the pool. My phone rang; it was my boss asking if I would like to do a Jaguar commercial in Seattle for two weeks. Jaguar, yeah like he really had to twist my arm.

Seattle was an interesting film shoot as it allowed me to wander around a lot of marinas and old boatyards. I met a few pipe smokers during those two weeks and even went on a couple boat rides. I didn't do any sailing but just being on any boat, trips my trigger.

Besides unloading the cars in the morning and loading back up in the evening I was free to explore. Years earlier I had been to the area many times but didn't have time to check out Puget Sound's variety of boats. To a boat nerd this place was nirvana, I seen more old wooden craft there than even in the Gulf of Mexico or the Great Lakes. I was also able to check out some wooden boat builders, being a wood worker myself, this was quite a treat. While walking down a street by the water I happened upon a wooden building that had most of their doors open. Inside two workers worked on the deck of a new wooden trawler they were building. I stood watching them for a while then an older gentleman came out and asked me if he could do something for me. No I said, just admiring the craftsmanship in their shop. I told him I enjoyed working with wood but was definitely not in the same class as the workers in this shop.

He introduced himself as Stan Bricker the owner of the shop. I was invited inside to look around and to check out the boat being built. The craft being built was a 60 footer, Stan told me they were sparing no expense on this build as the owner had expensive taste when it came to the exotic woods he wanted. He didn't want to use any paint where they could, instead use the colors in different woods.

Walking around the boat I noticed a very old easy chair by one of the work benches, I looked at Stan and at the same time we both said, pondering chair. We both laughed, knowing it's required when creating to sit and ponder on your project. Next to the chair was a small table with a jar of tobacco and a couple of pipes. I pulled a pipe out of my pocket and said me too.

We talked for a while and I told him I was from the Great Lakes. He had a great appreciation for some of the old wood boats that used to be made their. Stan then asked me what brought me to the Seattle area. When I told him about the different cars I hauled and at the moment I was on a film shoot for Jaguar he perked up and said follow me young man. We went outside to the parking lot behind the building and there sat a 50's vintage Jaguar SS120 drop top. These cars are like a work of art, to me nothing was finer than an E-Type but this was defiantly right up there in my book. My uncle, Miller Behrman had a nice workshop next to his house in Michigan that he restored older Jags so I was familiar with this model. Stan also had a later 70's vintage Jag XJ6 parked under a pavilion type structure that sat there and sparkled just like the 120 did. Both of us being fans of all things Jaguar we hit it off well, being a fellow pipe smoker helped also.

After touring the grounds some more it was time to pick up the cars, Stan was asking me all kinds of questions about the new Jags so I said why don't you come with me and you can speak with some of the folks from Jaguar, they are mostly Brits and a kick to talk to and besides they were quite passionate about Jags. We got into his 120 and went to the truck where I did my usual intense pre trip inspection. We went 20 miles or so to the location where the factory reps and film people were wrapping up for the day. Stan had never seen a commercial being filmed so he got a kick out of the enormity of equipment and people it took to accomplish the end result that in all actuality would end up being a 30 to 60 second spot during a broadcast of a select viewing audience being it was Jaguar.

Stan had a great time talking to the factory people and they also found him interesting as well. They invited us to have dinner with them so we could continue the conversation. Stan thought this was a gift from the automotive gods themselves. I loaded up the cars with Stan watching me; he had no idea of what all was involved in doing this and was generally interested in the process.

Back at the motel we got a table on the veranda and enjoyed a good meal and great conversation about cars, wood boats, and pipes as two of the Jag guys also smoked a pipe. The Jaguar guys were just as interested in what Stan did as he was about Jags. After a bit we all went over to Stan's shop where he gave them a tour of his shop and the boat he was currently building. It turned out to be a great evening although a late one. Stan invited me to the shop the next day, I gladly accepted as being at a wooden boat builders shop on the water was my idea of a great time indeed.

After my morning car thing I went back to the shop and met Stan's crew and volunteered to help in any way I could as I figured I'd pick up numerous wood working tips as these guys were master craftsmen. Always being one to gain more knowledge of that art I was all in. I've always been blessed with the ability to look at a piece of furniture and take a mental picture of it then go into my wood shop and build it with no plans, just the picture I had in head. I know that's a scary thought, but more times than not I wind up with a nice piece of furniture. I've never worked with a lot of exotic woods but look forward to it in the future. The rest of that second week I could be found in Stan's shop, every day was a valuable learning experience. A couple times we got together with the Jag guys for dinner. Our conversations were always without fail extremely interesting. Those two weeks spent there are truly treasured memories, as I've mentioned before listening to the tales of my elders is something very special, they wrote the book on whatever happened to be their passion and I was fortunate to hear it narrated right from the horse's mouth. The great wisdom and good old fashioned know how they possess is incomparable, I feel truly blessed to have met all of them that I have in all my travels.

Late in the fall of that year found me on the East Coast transporting Bentley's to just about every dealer in Florida. Bentley had come out with a new GT model that was all the rage. I found out from Monty the owner of the Rolls, Bentley dealer in Orlando that people were buying these cars for Christmas presents. Hmm I thought, a Bentley has been on my

Christmas wish list for many many years. Maybe I live in the wrong state or I've been ignorantly writing to the wrong Santa Claus. I've been working on that but to no avail yet, you know what they say, never give up hope or the ship so I keep dreaming. In my feeble mind dreams do in fact come true, they may take their own sweet time but it does happen. I guess it could be it boils down to priorities. If having an older Rolls or Bentley was on the top of my list I would find a way to have one, right now I'll settle for admiring and reading about them, as I take great pleasure in that alone, it works for me. I find it hard to imagine what it would be like to give someone a car for a gift let alone a Bentley GT. Sitting here writing about that I can't help but think about the exquisite people that Marc Dion writes about in his columns. They might not be the richest of folks but they are what built and made this country GREAT. I strongly recommend dear reader that you look Marc up on line and follow his column. I think of Marc Munroe Dion as our modern day Mark Twain he has the insight and a great and watchful eye on the pulse of the nation.

Traveling all over the country I would now and then see another driver smoking a pipe or cigar. Although they were few and far between. My buddy Dickey would smoke a cigar once in a while with me but he preferred Winston Lights. I quit sharing my cigars with fellow drivers as they didn't appreciate a good smoke and wouldn't know one if it crawled up their ass, they could never figure out how or why I got so much pleasure from a pipe or fine cigar. Whatever floats yer boat right?

I took quite a few exotic cars into Las Vegas and was able to go into most of the casinos around town. It was sure different from the 80's when you could drop your trailer and drive down the strip checking out all the sights. Trucks were no longer welcome in town, although I don't blame the town; I blame the uncouth way in which the drivers behave.

I've been fortunate that I never got bitten by the gambling bug, addiction, or urge to gamble. Many of the people I've worked with gambled whenever and wherever they could. Some drivers I know can sit in a casino all day or night, sometimes winning, other times not. In my feeble mind I could never justify throwing my hard earned money away, even if some do call it entertainment. While in Vegas for the first time in a semi I was at the Union 76 Truck Stop south of the strip where I was laid over for a night waiting on a load. There I met an old timer named Burt parked next to me; I was asking him about the strip as he told me he was familiar with Vegas. I had seen a few billboards advertising Prime Rib, Lobster and other delights for very little money. We decided to go into town and cash in on one of these dinners. My truck was detailed and looked great so I unhooked the trailer and off we went. We made a pass through town and decided to stop at the Sands for dinner. Walking into the casino Burt asked me if I gambled. No I said why throw my money away on that when I could use it to buy more chrome for my rig.

Glad to hear that he said, look around at all that you see. Do you think they built all these extravagant places by giving money away? Good point I said, and what about you? Hell no, I like to watch all the pretty women, eat at nice restaurants, and every now and then while in town I catch a band I like and enjoy the show. He said, now notice we have to walk through the casino gambling tables, one armed bandits and the like just to get to the good eats. The casino people want you stop and dump your cash before you get to the food, just keep walking Burt said. Sure enough that's exactly what we did. From that day on I never gambled more than 5 or 10 bucks at a time.

Vegas was a totally different city compared to what it was like 20 years before. It was kind of neat to deliver a Rolls Royce, Ferrari, or some other high end car to the casinos. If they let me park in their lot I'd go in and grab a great meal for a cheap price. Some of the casinos would have an in-house smoke shop where you could purchase a nice cigar to smoke as you emptied your pockets onto the tables of false hopes and broken dreams. I delivered three Bentleys and a Rolls Phantom to the Mirage one Friday and got permission to park for a while. I went into the

Mirage and looked around and learned that I could walk inside to the Luxor from there. Having gone by the place several times and seeing it on TV shows I was curious to see what it looked like on the inside.

From the Mirage I walked down the connecting shopping area between the two casinos. What an interesting walk that turned out to be. There were a few clothing shops I just had to check out. I like nice clothes; I even like shopping for them. I spent some of my teenage years working in a Men's Clothing store; I was the best dressed guy in school. Checking out these stores I was quickly reminded that I was completely out of my price range. Nice rags but way too much for me.

Venturing further I came upon a store that sold high end shaving accessories, well now this looked interesting, entering I started checking out the wares they had on display. Damn I never realized dragging a razor across your mug could be so expensive. They even had an area where you could get a shave. When at home I sometimes used a mug and brush to shave with so looking at their stock was interesting. The guy behind the counter was helpful in that he pointed out to me the fine benefits of using a genuine horse hair brush with the recommended soap and a fine straight razor or the faithful old ironsides that he assured me was made of the finest steel money could buy. Then of course you must accompany all that with your own personalized shaving mug for a mere 150 dollars. Inquiring further I was told that I could be set up with an entry level shaving kit for 250 dollars out the door, and that each time I shaved would be quite the exquisite experience indeed. Besides that, for just 300 more dollars my shaving enjoyment would be unsurpassed. I didn't quite grab onto this concept, I thought for that kind of money I'd better get a personnel arousal with a very happy ending, I damn sure didn't think I was going to achieve that with a razor.

I asked him if there was a tobacconist in the mall area, yup just keep heading towards the Luxor I was told. Further down the mall type corridor sure enough there was a cigar shop that had a few pipes in the window. From the outside it looked like something right out of a Dickens novel. Although it was new it sure looked old. Entering I was hit by that relaxing aroma of old wood and tobacco. Well now this is more like it I thought. Inside I was greeted by an older gentleman. right off the bat I just knew was a colorful character. I was right he introduced himself as Nelson we started talking while I looked around the shop, there were a few comfortable looking easy chairs in back by the humidor. Walking into the humidor I had an urge for a full bodied maduro. I took a mental inventory of what they had then picked out a dark Cameroon Torpedo by Punch. I figured I had a little over an hour to spare and this cigar would last about that long. Captain Jim always said you could mark off time with a cigar, meaning that if you smoked at a leisurely pace certain sizes lasted just so long.

Kicking back in a chair I learned that Nelson had migrated to Vegas from Fargo, North Dakota, he said he had to move before he froze to death in a very unforgiving Fargo winter. I was studying the various blends in jars when he told me about some of the more popular sellers. I picked out some blends that smelled interesting and a couple more cigars and was on my way again. I bypassed the other stores I went by as nothing really caught my attention.

For those of you that don't know, the Luxor is the casino you see advertised that looks like a pyramid. Inside it's quite a remarkable place. I walked around for a bit and enjoyed my cigar and checked out some of the exhibits. Whenever I'm in a casino I find it interesting to observe the expressions on the gamblers faces. Very few look happy or like their having a good time, most are sitting there clutching a cigarette with one hand while operating the machine with the other nursing or gulping their drink with a total look of desperation, want, and need on their face. I'd much rather read a book myself but that's just me, I'm sure the casino owners are glad there's not too many people like me around.

The next morning I loaded four test cars going to a high altitude test in Dillon, Colorado in the middle of the Rocky Mountains off of I-70. The route from Vegas to Dillon takes you up I-15 through Mesquite, Nevada. Then crossing into Utah I-15 runs you through a canyon for about 25 miles that's quite scenic, this stretch of road is one of the most picturesque drives in the country. Whenever I drove through canyons or areas that took my undivided attention I didn't smoke my pipe as with all the shifting, steering, and what not I needed both hands. Some guys just clamp their pipe in their mouth and carry on. I'm more inclined to not keep my pipe in my yap but hold it and enjoy it more. But like they say; each to his own. Sometimes running a canyon I would get my camera out and take numerous pictures, I never have developed the eye that some people have while taking photos. Getting to my destinations I'd look over the shots I had taken and they sure didn't have the scope or depth of the area I was after. I keep trying though, the pictures of cars, trucks, and boats I've taken usually turn out well but landscapes and people don't turn out so well.

After running the canyon it's a nice cruise up to I-70 where I head east across Utah then into the Rockies and on this run ultimately wind up in Dillon. Its runs like this where I really enjoy my pipes. Once up on I-70 you run east for a bit then you start seeing signs that tell you stop now, fill up, next services 150 miles. I love these stretches as it's just you and the road. On this trip I had stopped in Mesquite, Nevada at a Wall Mart to restock my fridge and grab other supplies like a case or two of water, munchies, and such. I wanted to stop at a rest area on I-70 to spend the night and cook diner. I bought the biggest steak they had and a one-time grill to cook it on. The spot I had in mind is in the middle of the no services area so in either direction its 75 miles to civilization east or west. Besides that all around you are some of Utah's famous red pictured rocks, cliffs and mountain peaks in the distance. I figured there would be a nice breeze blowing so I could shut my truck off for the night and enjoy my surroundings.

I kept at it all day stopping for fuel on I-70 and to check my tires and fluids before entering into no man's land. I got to the rest area around seven p.m. so that gave me a couple hours of daylight to grill my steak and enjoy the sunset while smoking my pipe. While setting up my grill an older couple pulled in with a huge RV that was decked out with all the bells and whistles. They had enough courtesy not to park right next to me but down 5 spaces or so. This RV was impressive; I was sitting on a picnic table assembling my grill with a corn cob pipe in my yap when they came out of their land yacht and started walking towards me. The guy put a pipe in his mouth and preceded to lite it on their way to where I sat.

Well now, I thought this should be interesting, a fellow pipe puffer way out here. They were from Mesa, Arizona. On their way to Glenwood Springs, Colorado then points east. They asked what I was going to grill, I said I just bought a steak at Wally World earlier that day and was about to grill it for a nice quiet diner in the middle of nowhere. They introduced themselves as Chet and Mary, and said they were about to do the same thing and would I care to join them. Sure I said, Chet helped me set up the grill then went to his RV and tossed some hickory chunks of wood onto the coals for better taste. Mary came out with a large tray loaded with three of the biggest porterhouse steaks I'd ever seen; these bad boys were two and a half inches thick. They made mine look like an afterthought. They told me to keep mine as diner was on them that night. Chet wanted to check out my rig as he had always been fascinated by semis. After giving him the ten cent tour he showed me his coach. Wow, this thing was really loaded; it had four pullouts and every creature comfort you could think of and then some. Chet grabbed a cooler and filled it with nice cold libations so we went back out to the picnic table while Mary made a salad. Come to find out Chet was a retired film editor from Los Angeles and had only been retired for a year, they both wanted to see the country while they were still able to enjoy it.

Me being a movie buff too we had a lot to talk about and the fact that I was familiar with film work the time flew by. The steaks were great, the scenery fantastic and the conversation interesting. They were two of the nicest people I have ever met on the road.

We started talking about pipes and different tobacco blends and traded some. Gazing at the sights around us with the sun setting in the distance was trance like. We were extremely lucky that we had the whole rest area to ourselves. The wind was just strong enough to keep us cool, and you could hear it blowing. Chet got up, went into his coach and came back with a small black box and a pouch of tobacco and handed both to me. He handed both to me saying, David I want you to have this, open the box. I opened it and inside were two beautiful Dunhill pipes, one a bent billard the other a strait billard with a fine medium dark finish. Holy shit I said, I can't accept these; they must cost a small fortune. No he said they didn't cost me a dime, they were a gift from a director and I think you should have them. Damn these pipes were brand new, never been smoked. I couldn't believe this, I thanked him over and over, I'd never smoked a Dunhill before and was anxious to find out if they were as good as I'd heard. Loading up the bent with some of his personally blended tobacco I lit it and was impressed.

The three of us sat there talking about movies, different actors and sets then the conversation switched to cars. Living where he did in Los Angeles and working at the studios Chet had seen his share of high dollar cars belonging to the stars and other Hollywood types. Chet was one of the few people that ever agreed with me that a Lamborghini Espada would make the perfect small family car. I mean think about it, it has four nice bucket seats, (man and wife in the front and two kids in the back) it looks very sporty, with V-12 power and still room for stuff in the boot. (Trunk) When you think about it wouldn't you rather drive that than an ugly no character minivan? I know I certainly would. We both agreed that the cookie cutter cars being produced were just down right blah! Another thing we had the same take on was the Pickups and SUV's people drive in the city and never took out of town let alone on dirt. Think about it, do people really need a ¾ or one ton dually to run around town in, never having anything heavier than golf clubs or groceries in the bed. And what about the high dollar SUV's with the brush guards over the lights and the fancy running boards. Don't forget the oversized wheels and tires. These types of people might drive over some gravel entering a parking lot and they think they're four wheelin. You have to admit, their fun to watch.

We sat there solving the counties transportation problems then started to talk about pipes again and of the pipe publications that used to be available. As we sat there puffing on our pipes I remembered the cartoons in Pipe Friendly magazine that depicted two or more dudes smoking their pipes and cigars out behind the garage as another guy kept an eye out for the smoking police. Both of us had seen those cartoons at the time and thought no, that will never happen. We looked at each other and said guess what, it's here. Isn't it strange that during the cigar boom in the 90's cigar smoking was so acceptable and now you're almost a criminal or worse?

It was getting on towards midnight so we called it a night and agreed on breakfast at 8:30 in the morning. I joined them in their motorhome the next morning then we ran together and talked on the CB until we got east of Grand Junction, Colorado to a truck stop and restaurant that's been in operation like forever. The food is great, the café is separate from the fuel pumps and store as it is an old log structure. After lunch we ran together to Glenwood Springs where they planned on spending a week or two.

I'm always amazed at the different people I meet on the road around the country. I try my best to get along with everyone I meet. I also try to find the good in people, most of the time people are friendly, but there are those that were just born pissed off. When I happen upon such folks I just give them a wide berth and leave them to their own misery.

From Glenwood Springs to Dillon on I-70 is one of the most scenic drives in the country. That stretch of road has been featured on History TV and others. I once watched a documentary on how they built it. I would have liked to have been on that construction project.

After meeting the test people at a motel and unloading the cars my company told me to get a room and sit tight for a few days while the test was being done and then to bring the cars back to Michigan. No problem I said, like they had to twist my arm. I can't remember the name of the motel but I was lucky and got a smoking room. I grabbed a couple bags from my rig then went to check out the room. Because I was with the test crew they had given me a suite with a balcony overlooking Lake Dillon. This lake is beautiful; the motel is on a mesa of sorts so I was high above it looking down. Well now I thought, this will damn sure work for a few days, and I can smoke in the room.

I settled in to a chair on the balcony and started looking through the attractions in the area; I noticed an advertisement for Barnes & Noble. Picking up my cell I called to get directions, I felt like a real ass, they were located 200 yards from the motel. Bookstores are very dangerous places for me to be, especially the bargain tables at Barnes & Noble. I was in need of new reading material so I walked over to check out what was new in the literary world.

The first section I go to in any bookstore anywhere in the country is the local history section. It's always interesting to read about the history of an area. Being in the Rockies this was doubly so, after all there was a good sized lake there too. Picking out a couple books on Lake Dillon and the surrounding area I noticed they were having a sale on audio books, damn I thought, maybe I should approach this with a frugal mind set. That lasted all of maybe 40 seconds; hey at least I had the thought even as fleeting as it was I still had to give myself credit for having it, right. John Grisham's book The Broker unabridged edition was there so I grabbed that and Joshua Slocums Sailing Around the World Alone. Then I went to the bargain tables, I did good on that venture as I only bought four bargain books. I knew I would drop many dollars that day and the days following in this establishment. (I'm always right about such things)

Walking back to the motel I spotted a pizza joint with tables outside so I went over, ordered a pie and started reading the local history enjoying one of my new Dunhill's. I was wearing a company shirt and another driver for another enclosed car carrier outfit recognized the logo on my shirt and introduced himself and we sat there and enjoyed a great pizza while discussing the ins and outs of what we did for a living.

During the next few days I explored Dillon and the lake and nearby Silverthorne. It took me a bit to get used to the altitude up there as the air is a tad thin. That area is one of my favorite in the country, the people are nice and the scenery is breath taking. I had a great time kicked back on my balcony smoking my pipe reading a good book, every few minutes I'd look out at the lake and surrounding mountains thinking how fortunate I was to be there, and being paid to boot.

The Dunhill pipes were definably good smoking pipes; I don't think their all that their cracked up to be but still a good smoke. Giving it some deep thought I probably wouldn't spend that kind of money for a pipe that was so lacking in character, don't get me wrong they are beautiful pipes although a bit plain for my taste. I appreciate all well-made pipes so having two Dunhill's in my eclectic collection to me is definitely a feather in my cap. I enjoy all of my pipes, some more than others depending on what time of year it is. Where I'm at in the country also influences what style or blend of tobacco I choose. I have tried to figure this out on more than a few occasions but have never been able to nail it down. What I have found is that the farther north I am the darker the blend, and vice versa in the south. When I'm in the more humid parts of the country I'll smoke a certain style of pipe, and then when in the arid states out west my taste in tobacco and pipes will change. Altitude will influence the burning qualities of certain blends too. Sometimes at very high altitude my pipe lighters won't work worth a damn, when that happens I revert to either Swan Matches from England or the good old trusty kitchen match. I like the Swan matches of old before they changed the striker material on the side. The new material when striking the match will sometimes send an ember to unwanted places that can have ill effects on your smoking pleasure. I've also experimented with the long specially made matches for lighting cigars but they too can cause a problem as the end of it will easily break off and land in unwanted places.

When trying to light up my pipe or stogie in breezy conditions I'll use my trusty pipe Zippo that I bought at Paul's Pipe Shop that has a picture of him on it. Although at first you can taste the lighter fluid it soon goes away. Some smokers I've observed will use these newfangled torch lighters with one to five separate blow torch type flames shooting out of them. I see this as a good way to burn the briar on a good pipe. Watching a newbie pipe or especially cigar guys try to light up with these torches is rather amusing to watch as they will burn a hole in their smoke or deform it in one way or another. I couldn't figure out for a long time why certain truck stop chains sold so many of this type of lighter, at the counter in the store part they would have what seemed like hundreds of them displayed. While standing in line checking some of them out I asked the clerk why they had so many and if they really sold that well, I mean how much flame does it really take to light a cigarette? The clerk and the driver behind me laughed and said they were used for lighting other smoking substances besides tobacco. I commented that surly it didn't take four flames to light a joint. No they told me, people use them to light their crack pipe and other drugs that people smoke, or to melt something to put in a syringe. Oh, I said and do you sell that many of them. Yup he said those and knifes at the counter sell like crazy. Walking back to my rig I gave this some serious thought. I've observed people standing in line and sure enough they will start handling the knifes and lighters and more times than not pick one out and purchase it with their other goods.

I was on a photo shoot for Honda and we were using a road that we needed police to direct traffic and mentioned this to one of the officers. He told me that I would be surprised at the number of people that bought that type of lighter. Many cars he pulled over would have these super torches lying on their counsel and that upon further inspection of the vehicle he would find other drug paraphernalia. This he said was not limited to any particular group of people, as in his experience it never ceased to amaze him how many different classes of people were using and abusing drugs. I suggested that maybe the manufacturers of these lighters were trying to appeal to the inner pyromaniac in people. Either way we both agreed that it was a scary way to live.

Whenever or wherever I would shut down at days end I fueled my truck as I figured anything could happen in the time I was sleeping or whatever waiting for my log book to jive so I could take off again. Years ago I pulled into a truck stop to spend the night thinking I would fuel in the morning as I had enough fuel for the night. The next morning I went inside to grab a coffee, reaching for the door I seen a sign that said they were out of fuel and wouldn't have any till that afternoon. I was stuck there waiting on a fuel delivery for several hours. That was the first and last time I ever put myself in that position. Waking up with full tanks gave me a range of around 800 or so miles to get to where I could top off again.

After fueling, drivers pull their rig forward a truck length then go inside to pay for or sign for their fuel, grab something to eat or whatever else they need then park for the night or head out again. After parking I would go inside to the restaurant if they had one or get fast food, go back to my truck and enjoy dashboard dinning for the evening. It's always entertaining to watch the action in the parking lot and to get a feel for what's happening or not happening around the place. Before I would call it a night I always did my paperwork for the day and made sure my log book was up to snuff for the next day. I usually smoked a cigar or pipe while doing this sitting in the driver's seat.

This enabled me to accomplish a few things at the same time. One, if some driver of questionable skill was attempting to park next to me I could get out and guide him and his or her rig in without them hitting me two, I wanted to see who and what type of people were walking around and what they were trying to sell or beg for. Three, if I didn't like what I was seeing I could go down the road to a more desirable place to spend the night. There's a lot of shit going down in these places that the more inexperienced driver has no clue of. Being aware of your surroundings and what types of characters are about is your first line of defense. I'm not saying all truck stops are like this but there are certain cities in the country that you better keep your guard up or you could be in deep shit. I could have been more comfortable back in the bunk doing my paperwork on a fold down desk but knowing what was happening around me was more important.

Something that bothers most drivers out there is the knock on the door late at night from some lot lizard (whore) asking if you want a date or to party. Getting awakened like that you never know for certain what's going on, there could be an emergency taking place, so you get out of your bunk to see what the deal is. Seeing some lizard standing next to your truck is never good in my book. Besides them, there are those who want to sell you something or need gas to get somewhere or money for food. You never know who might be knocking; some of these people are very convincing in their tales of woe. Most drivers in this day and age are not making the big bucks driving the big rigs as advertised on TV. They stay on the road and do what they can to help raise their families over the phone from all over the country.

As I mentioned, smoking a cigar or my pipe was a good way to relax while finishing up paperwork as that would end my day and the next hour or two would be mine to read a book or watch a movie. Whenever I smoked a cigar doing paperwork the sellers and lizards wouldn't hesitate to come up to my door and give their spiel of bullshit. But whenever I had a pipe in my mouth none of them ever approached my door. I would watch them start walking toward me and see me with pipe in hand or in mouth and suddenly keep walking. My pipe at times wouldn't even be lit, I'd just put it in the corner of my mouth and they would leave me alone. I found this most peculiar as this type of individual would normally have no reservations whatsoever about asking anybody for anything. It became a habit that I stuck a pipe in my yap while walking to and from the truck stop, while with pipe I was never, not once bothered by undesirable people asking for whatever. You can look at trucks all across the nation and see signs in their window telling approaching lot lizards or solicitors they are unwanted, I've never observed those signs doing any good at all, but my pipe worked very well.

I remember one instance quite clearly; I had to lay over a couple of days in Denver, Colorado to pick up some cars at The Mile High Stadium where Dodge was doing a ride and drive, from there the vehicles would be taken to the Phoenix Raceway where Nascar raced. While at the Sapp Brothers truck stop in town, I was on the phone talking to my mom when I spotted a lizard walking towards my truck. No I didn't have a pipe in my mouth. Anyway I told my mom a lot lizard was heading for the truck. The girl was skinny and tall and looked like she had been hung up wet more than a few times; she had on dirty short shorts, a tight top and no shoes. To walk across a truck stop parking lot with no shoes one had to have some tough feet, besides the fact that who knows what was on the lot. She jumped up on my running board and started her spiel of bullshit. As always I had on my headpiece for the phone. This girl was just getting into her groove with her story and my mom can here every word, then mom says, ask her if she knows Jesus, I did and she was floored, she stood there with her mouth open not knowing what to say. She looked around then back at me and said you've got to be kidding right? No I said, he can help you through prayer and faith. She gave me a look of total disbelief and contempt, got off the truck and started walking away while flipping me off. I yelled at her that Jesus saw that and was not happy with her. Then she used her other hand to salute me in stereo. I watched her go across the lot in search of a more understanding victim.

What I've always found enjoyable while traveling around the country is the diverse assortment of people in every part of the country whether it be north, south, east, or west or anywhere in between. Every part of the country and the folks inhabiting these different parts contribute something unique to the country as a whole which in the larger scheme of things allows us to be who we are. Granted that each part is partial to their neck of the woods but we are all after the common good of the nation. Sometimes it might be a blurred picture to some but in the end we're all in the same boat. Being able to see the wide variety of good that come from all over has amazed me. It's interesting to observe the different traditions and ways of life in all parts of the country. The same holds true with the tobacco we consume. Different strokes for different folks no matter where one might be.

Spending as much time as I have behind the wheel crossing and crisscrossing the U.S. in every which way possible while smoking my pipe has given me a lot of time to ponder about how we came to inhabit and develop every part of this nation. If you think about it, the U.S.A. compared to the rest of the world is like a young virgin, we haven't really been here that long. Other countries have tried to penetrate us but have never succeeded beyond our borders. That being said we must still watch our ass as there always seem to be those that want what we have or to change us. Hell, we're doing a good job of changing ourselves, what with all the do gooders shoving their nose where it doesn't belong. What gives Dudley Do Right the right to tell us where and when we can enjoy a smoke or not? I mean think about it, if these people want to do some good I'm sure there are many issues that need addressing with the same closed mindedness that they are attacking people that enjoy smoking. Just think of what could be accomplished if their energies were focused somewhere else. It seems to me that we have much bigger problems than people getting some pleasure out of a good smoke. God forbid someone should have a good time. Isn't diversity one of the things that make us great? If so why take it away from us with such hatred that they have? Maybe if we stood up for ourselves and fought back instead of taking it up the wazoo we would stand a better chance of enjoying it more in the future instead of having to hide behind a shed or in an ally. Food for thought eh.

Something else I was finding amusing delivering Personally Owned Vehicles (POV's) to people was how I got treated by the different types of people I delivered to. My company like others in the specialized auto transport industry moved cars for all manner of folks. From celebrities, pro athletes, the rich and wealthy, the car enthusiast extraordinaire, to the regular car guy that has always had a dream of owning a particular car. We did a lot of moves for athletes being traded to another team.

The wide variety of vehicles I moved was interesting to say the least. Being able to drive them on and off the trailer was fun. Some of the people I delivered to were uppity while others were friendly and grateful for the extra care we took while transporting their car. What I especially liked was taking a car to a real car person that couldn't wait for me to open the trailer so they could see their car. The look on their face was pure joy. Sometimes the vehicle would be a project car or truck and they couldn't wait to get it in their workshop or garage and get their hands on it. They were type of folks I could stand there and talk to for hours. Letting them talk and show off their workshop area was great, I got a lot of ideas for my dream garage. Some of the garages and work areas that I was shown were like taking a trip back in time. Old pictures and other auto memorabilia would not only be in the workshops but all through their house.

Some of the drivers I worked with liked to collect autographs and pictures of the stars and athletes we delivered to. I never got into that as many years ago I picked up an audio CD by Garrison Keillor and on it he explained that when meeting a celebrity you shouldn't act like an idiot and fawn all over them but to simply say you admire their work and tell them they are a credit to their profession. After all they are first and foremost people just like you and I. I've met quite a few famous people and had the opportunity to work with them on commercials and different sets and found this to be true. Delivering cars to celebrity's I would usually deal with one of their people and other times I dealt with them in person. I found all of them to be quite interesting especially if they were car people. I haven't met too many that smoked a pipe but a lot of them enjoyed a good cigar.

While waiting to pick up some show cars in Los Angeles one time I didn't have anything to do for three days while waiting and got a call from our Phoenix office telling me to make a quick trip to Beatty, Nevada and pick up a couple of test vehicles for Toyota. No sweat I told Emily one of our dispatchers. I thought that would be a nice trip through the desert instead of hanging around Ontario, California. The cars were scheduled to be picked up the next day at noon so I had plenty of time to get there, figuring out my time I really didn't want to go through Las Vegas during rush hour as I needed to go through town to get to 95 north to Beatty so I spent the night at Whisky Pete's in Prim, Nevada 30 miles west of town. (Remember the cows?)

I started off the next morning at around four in the morning avoiding the morning traffic. Arriving in Beatty early I stopped at a motel just north of town for breakfast. The place where I was to pick up was off on a small side street that was barely wide enough for my rig. Meeting my contact from Toyota he wanted me to back up and drive about 150 yards to a door on the building they were using. I wanted to load in the street but he said the cars were very sight sensitive and could not be seen in daylight. This was not uncommon as a lot of moves were considered sight sensitive. The driveway was an uneven dirt trail that I was skeptical about backing into. I wasn't worried about being able to get in there, what I was concerned about was the unevenness of the drive. The type of trailer I pulled had a door that was hinged on the bottom that I operated with hydraulics on the bottom side of the trailer. For this door to function properly it was best to be on level ground. I mentioned this to the factory guy but he was adamant the cars not be seen. OK I said let's give it a try. After backing up and getting in position I went back and started letting the door down. Whack, the hydraulic ram on the right side broke loose from the weld and tore the shit out of things, so here I was 120 miles north of Vegas with a major welding job needing to be done before I could do anything. Well now, aint this a bitch I say to Greg the dude from Toyota. We need a welder I tell him. After conferring what all needed to be done we jumped in his car and went in search of someplace to get the work done. What I was grateful for was the fact that I could still pull the trailer down the road instead of calling a mobile welder out. You need to understand that Beatty, Nevada is in the middle of the desert and isn't all that big and as far as repair shops go they were none existent when it came to the type of work I needed done. We went to an auto salvage yard thinking they had a welder or would know of someplace that could do the work. The guy's at the salvage yard said they had cutting torches but no welder. Then an old timer came out and said just maybe a guy north of town might be able to help us out. He said the guy's name was Marvin Walker and that he had a Quonset hut next to his house and that he did welding for a hobby.

Off we went in search of Mr. Walker, we found him in his shop grinding away on a piece of steel for something. Looking around his shop I spotted an old pipe and a can of Captain Black on a work bench, besides all the steel stock he had lying about I figured he could do the job and that we were in good hands. Marvin Walker could be a twin to Henry Fonda with the same wit. We introduced ourselves and Marvin said he'd be glad to help us out if I could get my rig backed up to his shop. This was no easy feat as I would have to back in 100 or so yards off of US-95 up and over and through a cattle guard then blind side the rig around a group of tree's and up to the shop, total distance more than a third of a mile. I told Greg it was worth a shot after surveying the situation for a few minutes. The only thing I could do was to get the rig and give it a try.

Once back ay Marvin's I showed him what needed to be done and then with his and Greg's help I backed the rig up to the shop and we were in business. First he cut out all the torn metal then we went looking around his piles of stock for the right gage of steel to fabricate a new bracket assembly.

We learned that Marvin had retired as the drain and water commissioner in Beatty and that he loved to putter around in his shop doing the odd welding job now and then for the folks in the area. There was all manner of old equipment around the side and back of the shop that Greg and I started looking over then Marvin called out to us to keep an eye out for snakes. A few minutes after that as we were looking over a very old dozer a Rattle Snake about three and a half feet long took off from under the dozer blade. This thing wasn't all that long as far as desert snakes go but it had a girth of about ten to twelve inches and looked powerful. Damn I said that thing could ruin your day. We went around to the front of the shop and looked around there; I was looking across the road and seen an old twin engine plane sitting among the brush and tumble weeds. Well I'll be damned I said, that sonofabitch is still there. Back in the 80's when I hauled lumber into Vegas or points south of there I had heard a rumor that it was a drug plane that crash landed there, another story told was that it was a few rich guys looking for a cathouse. This could be true as behind there set back from the road was indeed a whorehouse. I can't remember for sure if it was called Fran's Ranch or the Cotton Tail Ranch, either way I remember the rumors surrounding the place. The plane looked just as it did twenty some years ago. They say that the desert is timeless, in more ways than one this holds true.

Marvin did a fantastic job of fabricating new brackets and supports. I've always considered myself to be a better than average welder and pretty good with a cutting torch. Compared to Marvin my work looked like a pre-schooler. Testing the door out it worked better than it ever had. I knew that Marvin being a pipe smoker would give the repair job much thought and contemplation and that the work would be far superior to any repair shop. How right I was. I paid Marvin what he wanted plus a healthy tip, and when I got back to my yard in Michigan I mailed him a couple of company shirts and a hat. To this day I still send Marvin a Christmas card.

Having loaded the cars in Beatty I delivered them to Torrance, California the next day then made my other pickup in fine fashion. As I've mentioned before, the interesting people I meet in my travels never ceases to amaze me. If not for Marvin and his artistic talents with steel and welding I would have been stuck in Beatty or would have had to return to Vegas and probably would have wound up with a half assed job that would have lasted maybe a week. Besides that I would have missed my scheduled pickup appointment in Los Angeles. Never a good thing when several companies are counting on your timely arrival.

Being a specialized automotive carrier I was able to be off the beaten path that a normal 18 wheeler was confined to. One of the things I was fanatical about was the appearance of my rig, when I say that I mean every inch of it. One of my interests was always being on the lookout for different types of waxes, aluminum polish, and tire dressing. I never considered my rig clean unless my tires were dressed. You need to understand that taking an applicator and wiping the tires on an 18 wheeler is a bit more work than doing it to a four wheeler. The quest for a better product to accomplish this was always fun. I even mixed different products together to come up with my own special waxes and such, just like I did with blending different tobaccos together. Operating a rig that shined like new also opened doors for me and allowed me to meet interesting people anywhere I traveled. Wherever I went folks would more times than not compliment me on how great my rig looked. I found this to be helpful in the fact that I could get away with parking (positioning) my rig in areas that trucks were not usually allowed to be. This came in quite handy in my never ending search for tobacco shops, book stores, and marinas. I was told a long time ago to take pride in your ride know matter what it is. Besides the many benefits of a shiny rig, keeping it all polished I could stay in better shape. I could always tell when I gained a pound or two as working in such tight quarters in the trailer I did a lot of squeezing in and around the vehicles, there wasn't much room in there especially with larger vehicles. More times than not I would have to get in and out buy crawling through one of the windows, it was much easier that way instead of trying to get out through the door, at times there were only a couple of inches of clearance to work with.

I always kept a pipe and tobacco in the trailer to sit and contemplate how I was going to load my vehicles, my pipe let me think things through instead of just going for it and having to possibly reload or scratch a car. I always took the same care in handling a vehicle whether it be a Rolls, Corvette, or an auction car someone had their heart set on. Taking the extra time to enjoy my pipe while mulling over my options saved me a lot of unwanted grief.

Transporting specialized autos sounds like it would be an easy job, but it's not, I worked my ass off making sure everything fit and wouldn't bounce into another car or deck. I spent a lot of time crawling and climbing, most days I felt like a monkey. That's not entirely a bad thing as it kept me in shape the same as if not better than if I went to a gym everyday such as my dad does. Hell, he's 80 years old and without fail is working out at the gym every morning at 5:30 a.m.

CHAPTER VIII

CHANGES

The atmosphere of the road that I once knew was changing drastically, and not so much for the good. I remember when I first started running over the road you needed to have experience, before a company cut you loose with a truck to go to neighboring states or across the country you had to know what you were doing. This was proving to be not the case anymore. Companies started hiring what I called foggers, if you held a small mirror in front of a prospective drivers face and they could breathe on it and create a fog they would send this person through their school for a week or two and give them a certificate claiming they were fit to operate an 18 wheeler. I started to seriously question my choice of profession. One of the reasons that I changed the types of equipment and commodities I hauled was to gain more experience to become a better driver. At one time this proved to be beneficial but not so any longer as this new breed they were sending out on the road has no earthly clue as to what they are doing. Where there once used to be professional etiquette among drivers and just plain common sense, that has suddenly been tossed out the window so to speak.

I have met quite a few people that have attended the truck driver schools and turned out to be excellent drivers, they genuinely strived for and wanted to be professional. Then on the other hand there are those who don't give a damn about how they operate their equipment or the effects their actions have on others sharing the road with them, not to mention what they lack in portraying a professional image. I mean it doesn't take a lot of brain power to understand that if you want to be treated like a professional you might want to act and dress as one. I was raised to always be as neat and clean as I could be no matter what I was doing. If you look and act like dumb ass, you'll be treated as such. I'm truly embarrassed buy some of these individuals driving rigs in this ever changing world in which we are all trying to survive. I must admit though, as I watch this new breed of driver that they are very comical to watch. They can be a great source of entertainment, especially when I'm shut down for the night doing my paperwork and watching them trying to maneuver around a parking lot. Sadly I miss the courtesy of old when you could count on the actions of others being more thoughtful.

One of the things I miss is the truck stop of not too long ago where you could find what you needed in the store part and the restaurants that served actual recognizable food. I've been in some places what they served I would have second thoughts about, feeding their food or what they want you to think of as food to my dog. As far as trying it eat healthy on the road forget it, how can you keep an eye on your waistline when you scarf down a three pound burrito every night. My good friend and fellow driver David Vesconi always without fail orders his food just like he wants it prepared, his son being a chef might have something to do with it, I've even seen him walk back to the kitchen and speak with the cook. If more people would do that maybe things could change.

What used to be called Truck-Stops are now called Travel Centers. Where a driver used to be able to sit down, order an enjoyable meal and relax with a smoke afterwards is no longer possible. We were in the old days able to purchase pipe tobacco or a decent cigar at a truck-stop is no more. About the only thing that has been improved upon is the coffee now available. I like my java strong, like stand a spoon up in it strong while others like it bit more civilized. Most stops now offer seven or more different blends. If there were more pipe smokers out there maybe they could do the same with tobacco. One can choose from any brand of cigarettes or flavored cigars such as grape ape, very Vera vanilla, or most any other candy assed flavor you may think of. If one is going to smoke tobacco, why don't you want to taste it!

There are exceptional truck-stops located around the country where you can get more of the things needed to make life on the road more enjoyable but for the most part all you get is a carbon copy just like all the rest of the interchangeable pods throughout the land. As many times as I've been to these places I could be blindfolded and still find exactly what I wanted in anyone of them anywhere in the country. Giving it some thought maybe the corporations don't wish to confuse the majority of mental midgets traveling about. Us pipe smokers can thank our lucky stars that Tobacconist Shops have their own personality.

While we're on the subject of changes, I pulled into Barstow, California late one afternoon in August with a scheduled pick-up in Long Beach the next day. I had heard rumors of a new law that prohibited trucks from idling and that the tickets being issued for such criminal negligent activity was upwards of 250 dollars for the first offence and went up drastically for second and third offences.

Anyway, having some extra time and with nightfall a ways off I figured in my feeble mind this would be an excellent time to do some preventive maintenance work inside my trailer. The decks in the trailer are adjusted by hydraulic rams attached to square steel guides and supports, the guides work much easier when they have a coat of graphite on them and you needed to keep up with keeping them properly coated or the decks would chatter when raising them up and down. Never a good thing when you're adjusting a car worth 300 grand or more. I needed to keep the truck engine running so I could keep the PTO (power take off) engaged to operate the hydraulics. The rear door was folded down and side door latched open for air flow as the outside air temperature was over 100 degrees, inside the trailer read 118 degrees. There I was minding my own business painting graphite on my supports WORKING to make my job easier and safer. As I turned around to do another support this cop pokes his head in and wants my credentials, why I ask him, because you are in violation of the no idle law he tells me. Well now, this creates a bit of a difference of opinion I say, I am working, becoming one with my equipment improving my quality of work for the betterment of all mankind. For some reason unbeknown to me he failed to get the point or see the hummer in my comment. He went on to inform me with a straight face that California law prohibited the idling of trucks for more than 5 minutes and that he was going to issue me a citation. I argued the fact that I was working, and needed my engine running to operate my hydraulics to accomplish my task at hand. We stood there arguing who was right for quite a few minutes when I noticed his trooper car was still running and I could smell the exhaust of an engine in need of a tune up or the graveyard and I brought this to his attention. By this time a crowd was starting to gather to observe what was happening. I knew without a doubt I was right and I wasn't about to let this ass of a cop write me a ticket for trying to do my job. As far as I was concerned this cop was corrupt and when the law is corrupt there is no law. Just when I was about to put the whole shoe store in my mouth by telling him that, the manager of the truck-stop told him to get the hell out of HIS parking lot and if he thought he needed a cop he would call upon them, otherwise stay out and stop harassing the drivers. Needless to say said cop wasn't too happy right then with a gathering crowd of 30 plus drivers and the manager ready to back me up. After the cop left I listened to other drivers tell me that a driver alone in his cab cannot keep their truck running to use the AC or heater but, if you had a pet in the cab with you it was OK. I found out that if you threatened to call the animal rights people they would fight your ticket on the grounds of cruelty to animals. Well doesn't that make a lot of sense, and what about the driver I ask? Too damn bad was the answer as far as the law was concerned. The safety of the driver and all those who share the road with him or her depends on the quality of rest they get. How in the world are you supposed to get quality sleep when it's hot or cold?

I went into the truck-stop when I was done and kept my truck running, as I have ever since. Some laws were just meant to be broken.

Three weeks after that episode I was back in the Los Angeles area on my way up the 405 from Irvine to pick up two Rollers in Ventura. I was cruising along minding my own business when I observed flashing lights in my mirror, now what the hell does he want I thought. My rig and I were spic and span clean and shiny, when you look right in California you don't usually get messed with but apparently nobody informed this cop of this unwritten rule of thumb. My log book was up to the date, I last changed my duty status so that was good and my fuel recites matched my log book for once, I felt pretty good about that as for me this was way beyond the call of normal duty. Besides that I wasn't speeding and I happened to be using the proper lanes. I thought things were going quite well as traffic that day was light and I was smoking a new blend that I had given a vast amount of thought to and had aged for a few months that turned out to be more enjoyable than I anticipated. I pulled onto the shoulder and stopped, in the old days you would walk back to cop car. Not so anymore, they come to you and stand on your passenger side running board. I rolled down the window for mister CHP (California Highway Patrol) and awaited his arrival with great anticipation as for once I didn't think I had done anything wrong. Figuring he would ask for all my paperwork I had it ready when he climbed onto my truck and poked his head in the window.

Top of the morning to ya I said with a smile that wasn't quite genuine. Same to you driver any idea as to why I pulled you over? Nope, I haven't an earthly clue I informed him. I started to hand him my papers and log book when he said, if your paperwork looks as good as your truck you're OK, is it? Sure is I say, he then looked on top of my dash at my pipe. He then informed me that a new California law was going into effect that banned people from smoking in a work environment and that in the future some other cop could issue me a citation for doing so as the inside of my cab was considered a work environment. It took me a minute to comprehend this information as in my wildest dreams I never saw this coming. I looked at him then out the windshield then back at him and said, no shit are you serious? Yeah no shit driver, the pipe your smoking grabs attention and you could get a ticket in the future. He said that his grandfather and father and he smoked a pipe and that he was just giving me a heads up to what was coming down the pike in the not too distant future. We talked for a few more minutes and bid each other farewell. I appreciated him telling me about this new costopo law. I thought damn I spend a lot of time behind the wheel in this state and if the rest of the country follows suite this could really suck. I gave this considerable thought the rest of the way to Ventura, the only thing I came up with was that the inside of my cab and trailer were MY work spaces and that I could argue that point. Besides, I was more or less a one man show because I loaded and unloaded this thing myself and I was the Captain of this ship. Nobody besides me had any business on or in my ship so screw them and their new law I thought. When, or will it ever end with the amount of control different states and the government as a whole would let us smoke in peace and harmony with all that is good and holy to a cigar and pipe smoker.

Over the next few days I mentioned this to other drivers and some became quite livid that they wouldn't be allowed to smoke in their trucks. I would be able to wrap my head around this law if I shared my work space with others but I don't, so I really don't see the logic in it other than the fact that it's just another form of revenue for states that are in need of cash.

Another thing I find amusing is the fact that every other month there seems to be another new law taking effect that makes our jobs as drivers more difficult and a bigger pain in the ass to deal with. I mean think about it, without trucks this whole world stops period. Everything you touch, drive, eat, wear, live in, or what have you has been brought to you and made available to you by the men and women on the road throughout the world driving trucks so you can enjoy your life and consume and acquire more shit. I hear people complain about so many trucks being on the road and they're too ignorant and shallow to understand that the world works because of the fact that things get transported by trucks. Without us the trains couldn't operate, the ships couldn't cross oceans and the people would starve to death. I remember watching a news clip years ago when they showed Janet Reno standing in front of a multitude of microphones spewing forth her words of infinite wisdom wanting to know just what all those smoke belching trucks are doing out there, and that there is no need for them to be there at all. We as the American people need to put a stop to this nonsense. In short she wanted all trucks off the American roads as we were in the way, belching smoke creating traffic jams and in general didn't need to be out there. Talk about out there, she takes the cake. While watching this crazy dyke looking mean bitch talking I can truthfully say that I have never seen anyone in such dire need of an orgasm in my life as she seemed to be. I mean really, isn't there some pour demented soul out there willing to step up and take one for the team and the good of all mankind and give this loony broad some relief? What really blows my mind is that WE as the American people elect these dimwitted schmucks to appoint dimmer witted schmucks to tell us how to live. Is it just me or is our system failing us?

Not long after that I happened to be some place where their radio was tuned to Rush Limbaue and he was telling his audience that there was just too much consuming going on. I didn't hear what he said before or after so I can't comment on his point without knowing what it was but I hope he was saying it in jest. Isn't that why most people work and keep working, so that they and their families can consume and acquire stuff and live a better life?

Like the smoking laws that get passed and laid upon us so it is with my chosen profession, between the government and the different states imposing new laws every day that make it harder for us to do our jobs I see the quality of life that my profession once provided being flushed right down the crapper. If one thinks about it the truck drivers of this nation alone could stop the entire industrialized world if we had the right leadership and could stick together. In short, if we stop, the world stops no ifs and or buts about it. There was a scene in the movie Hoffa that I will never forget and to this day must scare the hell out of companies the world over. John Kennedy our president was in an elevator with his brother Robert and they were discussing Jimmy Hoffa and the teamsters organizing the truck drivers. John looks at Robert and says, can you imagine if all the drivers in the country were organized? If you read between the lines you can see what happened from there.

Granted some changes are good and others not so much. I hear about all the new laws governing where and when we can smoke and can't help but wonder when enough is enough. Why is it that our government wants to or feels the need to dictate what we can and cannot enjoy. Another thing that baffles me is the power of just one ninny, if a group of people are sitting around smoking a pipe, cigar or whatever, one ninny can speak up and voice their unhappiness with said smokers and although in a vote the ninny would be out numbered ten to one the ninny will get their way. What happened to the democratic society that we are supposedly living in? It sure seems like it is slip sliding away more quickly than we are comfortable with. As Marc Dion has expressed in his column more than once people in other counties that are unhappy with what their governments are doing they damn sure let them know about it in a not so subtle way. When we do that here they bring out the National Guard and shoot us with tear gas, rubber or lead bullets to control us in the manner in which they see fit. We as a people elected these people. In my humble opinion we have too many people in government that need to justify their existence and jobs by making laws about things they know nothing about.

Another change I'm unhappy about but fortunately can do something about is getting older. They say that you are as old as you feel or think. Most days I don't feel as old as I am but then on others I wake up and wonder why I ache all over. When that happens I pop a couple Aleve and in a short time feel good as new or as close to it as my 57 year old body can. Speaking of getting old, after I picked those two Rollers (Rolls Royce) up in Ventura I was heading up I-5 north of Sacramento around dusk on my way to Seattle. I had the radio on listening to some good old rock and roll smoking my pipe enjoying the drive when this car load of people started to pass me then for some reason they began to slow down when they were half way past my trailer. Not thinking too much about it as some people get a tad skittish while passing a big rig I thought they'd get around me in a minute or two. They eased up on me and just kind of hung by my cab, wondering what was up I glanced down at this car which was filled with what looked to be young coeds mucking about inside, the car was a pristine 70's vintage Buick Vista Cruiser station wagon, not a very common site in these days of Mini Vans and SUVs. I was paying more attention to the car than I was to what was going on in it, upon closer inspection I noticed this thing was filled with girls even in the far rear fold down seats. They then honked their horn a couple times and pulled ahead a couple car lengths and while I was still looking at the car I finally noticed I was being flashed by most occupants in the wagon. Well, holy tits on a Ritz, I just got flashed by a car load of girls and didn't realize it till the show was over. Damn I thought, am I getting that old or am I just a hopeless car guy? I prefer to think I'm more the later. For a long time I didn't tell my fellow drivers about this for fear of being tossed out of the true truck driver club. After all we do have a rather unscrupulous reputation to uphold.

While I'm on that subject, sitting up as high as we do in our rigs you do see some crazy things going on in passenger vehicles. Back in the day drivers used to take an amber colored cone shaped clearance light and cut the end off then glue the end of a clear light on the end and insert a bigger bulb into it and mount it on the lower arm of their mirror with its own switch inside so they could turn it on and off as the DOT frowned on such lights. These lights would act as a mini spot light and if positioned just right would shine into the car passing you affording you a nice lit up view of what the occupants in the car were or were not doing. I never got around to installing one of those but I've heard plenty of stories about the goings on in other vehicles at night. Over the years I have observed some very amusing things but I'll put them in my next book. Trust me when I say that chapter will be entertaining, like beyond far out. I'll even share some stories of what some of my friends have witnessed. Stay tuned dear reader.

CHAPTER IX

THE CONTEST

When I returned to Michigan after that trip I decided it was time for a break from the road and felt like hanging around the Mitten State for bit. Captain Jim and I started getting together again for our Sunday Night smoke. One day that fall in the year 2007 if my memory serves me right (as I've mentioned before this is not always the case) we went to The Common Grill in Chelsea Michigan for a nice meal in Jims opinion, this place is the best restaurant in the state to eat. According to him it's rated third in the state. I must agree with him as the food is very good, and the service is always exceptional. I too enjoy going there as down the street from the grill is Mule Skinner Boots. I've always had a thing for nice boots, like the pipe or book that just feels right in your hand so do a fine pair of boots feel on your feet. For me, unlike a vast majority of people having the proper footwear for whatever occasion is important. Having the right boots has served me well through the years, besides saving my feet from injury or a bad slip; much like an automobile tire, the right traction is important.

While enjoying a great meal we were discussing pipes when Jim informed me that in the latest news letter from The Arrowhead Pipe Club the pipe contest and show/swap meet was in two weeks and would be held in Michigan that year. We talked it over for a bit and decided to attend as Paul was getting up there in years and this would be one of the last times we might see him at an event.

After we ate we went to the boot joint where I spent more than I had intended to but I acquired some fine boots. Leaving town we decided to swing by East Lansing to drop in on Doug at Campbell's Red Door smoke shop as both of us needed a few items. Besides we had to see what was new and improved, we both needed to resupply our stash of Oliver Twist and the Red Door was the only place in the area to get it. We had taken Jims Vette and had a nice drive up to East Lansing via the back roads.

Arriving at Doug's both of us bought a nice tasty dark cigar and settled into the chairs in front to enjoy the scenery outside. (Remember this place is on campus) We might be getting older but that doesn't mean we're dead, like they say, just because you're on a diet doesn't mean you can't read the menu. Besides right next to the table and chairs Doug has a rack filled with past issues of Pipes and Tobacco magazines along with Smoke and Cigar Aficionado magazines. Being on the road as I had been for the past few years I had missed a few copies. Another thing about sitting in the Red Door as I mentioned earlier is the diverse arrival of folks who frequent the place. I was meandering around looking at their new array of pipes when I noticed Doug had a sale on tinned tobacco, among the offerings I spied a stack of Benjamin Hartwell Private Reserve, I read the description on each of the different tins and settled on a couple tins of Evening Stroll, and a few others that looked promising. We spent about an hour and a half at Campbell's then hit the road for home. On the way I tried some of the Evening Stroll and was quite pleasantly surprised at the smoothness of it. I know some of the purists reading this would turn their nose up at the thought of smoking an aromatic blend I'm not all that biased in my selection of tobacco. Jim gave it a try and gave it a thumb's up also.

Two weeks later Jim and I went to the pipe contest held in a suburb west of Flint, Michigan and yes Paul our Stately

Grand Wizard of Pipedom was there to oversee the event. Walking into the venue I was surprised to see some of the club members that I haven't seen in a few years and was glad to see they were still involved with all things pipe. I hadn't seen Paul in a few years and it was nice catching up with him. Around the outside of the fairly large room this was taking place in were the prizes that could be won if you placed well enough in the contest. I gave my attention to the prizes towards the rear as in the past I've looked closely more towards the bigger prizes in front and have bombed out early much to my disappointment. I chose my trusty Paul's Cayuga bent that I have always used in the past in contests as Paul will throw in a bonus if you win smoking one of his pipes. On one of the display tables were several pipes that you could possibly win with the purchase of raffle tickets that would be drawn after the contest. These were some very nice pipes and would be considered a plus in anyone's collection. I bought as many tickets as I deemed rational. Then I wandered around to the tables where the venders had set up their products and drooled over some of the more interesting pipes. One of the venders had half a table covered with pipes that the briar was covered with a cork material that he said gave you a nice cool smoke. (Wish I had a dollar for every time someone proclaimed that in their advertisement) These pipes looked unique with a lot of character; I was a bit concerned with what they would look like after continued use with the effects of your hand on the cork. They had so much character though in fact it didn't detour me from purchasing a nice bent that seemed to be calling out, take me home Dave you won't regret it, I did and I haven't regretted it!

Not long after that the contest started, it had been quite a few years since I'd been in a contest and I didn't have a clue as to how well I would do. For some reason Jim decided to set this one out as he was having a fine time talking to the vendors and meandering about checking out the wares available. There looked to be some experienced smokers that I guessed had a lot more pipe smoking finesse than I possessed. To be truthful I'd be happy just to not be the first one out. For some unknown reason I just seemed to get in a groove type trance, much as I do when I'm knocking down some serious miles in my rig. It's rather difficult to explain but while I'm in that zone I just relax quite a bit and things are much smoother. I was looking over my new cork hybrid pipe and trying not to puff too much and at the same time keep a good bit of ember burning but not too much. Surprisingly some of the guys that I thought would be the stiffest competition started to fall out earlier than I had anticipated. Hmm I thought this to be most interesting, and then a few more dropped out. The seconds and minutes were dragging on with every puff I thought it would be my last, but as long as I was still blowing smoke I still had a chance. I tried to stay in my zone and keep a somewhat cavalier attitude as this was all in fun right. Wrong, the more smokers that dropped out the better my chances were becoming of placing in the top order of things. As this would be one of the last if not the last contest I'd be in with Paul I desperately wanted to place well. The next 20 minutes sorted out more contestants, then things seemed to level off a bit and low and behold I was still in the running. Yeah, this was a surprise to me too as I never dreamed I could last this long. (Isn't that every guy's dream?) I figured if things kept going the way they were this could shape up to be a quite nice finish indeed. I sat there contently smoking slowly contemplating other activities where some of the same performance aspects could be applied. See it's not only pipe smoking that these thoughts cum into play. We pipe smokers are a considerate lot.

More time passed with several more puffers dropping out and then it was down to five. I couldn't believe this, I was still in it. Number five dropped out then shortly after number four went by the wayside. Damn only three of us left, I slowed down as much as I dared still in shock that I was still blowing smoke for a few minutes more when I puffed my last bit of smoke. Just after I called out my number and said out, the guy sitting at the next table called out. The last guy in was Tom from the Lansing Pipe Club, he was smoking a Meerschaum bent that looked to be a nice pipe. I thought coming in third was great, although I didn't win in my mind I was more than happy to get a podium finish. There again this holds true in many activities. After it was over I got to stand with Paul and the other two and get pictures taken and receive my winnings for third place which turned out to be four pipes and quite a bit of tobacco and other pipe accouterments. Then they started to draw the tickets for the different prizes I mentioned earlier and this must have been my lucky day as my numbers were called three times. In the past whenever I entered a drawing I never won a thing and for that matter I haven't won anything since. Although I do remember one time a few years later meeting some drivers in a casino in Reno and sliding a five dollar bill into a video poker machine and winning a hundred bucks and instead of dumping it back in the machine I cashed out and left.

Getting back to Jims we had a smoke and tried out some of the tobacco I had won which turned out to be quite good. One of them being a box of pouches of Troost Pipe tobacco which I had never tried but Jim had and it was better than I expected.

I came away with eight new pipes that day, seven I had won, two of which were Canadians and two free hands one of which was a Nording and is one of my favorite pipes to this day. I had never been into Canadians all that much but Jim swore by them telling me that once I tried one it would become a favorite and as usual he was right. The cork pipe I bought that day was indeed a cool smoker, when I returned to the road I smoked it every other day allowing it a day to dry out between smokes.

The following week I started to write. I've always wanted to write about my experiences driving all over the country and about the people I've met along the way, being out and about as I have my take on different areas of the country in my mind is a bit more in depth compared to say someone that has taken a vacation and returns home and writes about it. Besides having lived in so many different parts of the United States, I got to know the people who lived there. Another aspect I always thought unique was all the types of driving I've done and totally different commodities I've hauled. As mentioned earlier I've always wanted to write so with those thoughts in mind I gave it a try. Was I ever in for a surprise, what I figured to be an easy task, completely floored me. I would be writing away and then like a cold towel to the face I would hit a thing I became quite well acquainted with called writers block, I started to despise this thing that would not allow me to get anything down and what I did write when I re-read it sounded like complete and utter shit. When that happened which it did more times than I like to admit I would go to Schuler's Books in Okemos, Michigan where I was living at the time and sit in one of their easy chairs and read a book for inspiration. If I wasn't there I could be found in Barnes & Noble in East Lansing just a couple blocks from Campbell's Red Door tobacco shop.

Often when I got into one of these blocked moods I went to Jims in Howell and we would hash over what was holding me up or why what I wanted to say wasn't coming out as I wanted. If that didn't work I would go back to reading. Sometimes I think I'm possessed with reading, I mean I read constantly. My interests cover such a wide spectrum that I never cease to be amazed at the enormity of books out there that I find entertaining. I can't for a moment think of what life for me would be like if I couldn't read. I was fortunate to be born into a family of readers. My grandparents read a lot as do my parents and sisters. I'm the type of person that goes on vacation and reads a book, I can probably count on my hands how many times I've went to bed in my life without reading a book before dozing off.

I get the same feeling walking into a bookstore as I do entering a Tobacconist shop. I really dig the comfortable feeling I get. I'm often asked by people why I read so much and my answer to them is the question, why don't you, reading can teach you anything and take you anywhere you want to be.

CHAPTER X

AUTORAMA DETROIT

While I was experiencing one of my blocked phases Jim and I were having one of our Sunday night smokes watching 60 Minutes when we made plans to go to Autorama the next weekend. For those out there that don't know about Autorama, it's a Hot Rodders paradise. Every and anything relating to hot rods, street machines, customs, and muscle cars can be found at this event. This show is held at Cobo Hall right on the Detroit River in downtown Detroit. It's held in the second or third week in February every year about a month after the North American Auto Show which is held at the same place.

Just arriving at Cobo is interesting as most everyone attending parks on the roof of Cobo Center, getting that many gear heads together is a trip. Even though it's held in the winter you'll see just about every car parked on the roof detailed. Jim being involved with the United Street Machine Association as he has been for many years he knows quite a few people there displaying their rides. Meandering around looking at all the cool rides is great when you get to meet the builders of the cars.

This year we took a friend of mine from the Lansing area Max Solomon who is also quite a gear head along with his dad. His dad is retired and cruises around in a 1949 customized bright yellow Ford Pick-up and a new Corvette drop top. My dad cruises around in a Cadillac XLR which is Cadillac's version of the Vette. Max had never been to this show and for him to be there with someone that knew most of the people there was a real treat for him.

We walked around looking at all the cool assed cars then decided to take the people mover (mono rail) to Greek Town for lunch and to have a bowl of pipe while there. Greek Town in Detroit has the greatest Chicago Style deep dish pizza I've ever had. Upon returning to Cobo we were at one end of the second or main floor when we came upon this huge display for Reliable Carriers, they are the biggest and best specialized auto carriers in the country. They had a hot rod Peterbuilt there that was truly awesome; this thing was Omaha Orange which is the companies color. The name of it was Rock Bottom and was stretched, lowered, chopped, and just plain cool, especially if you're into trucks, the doors where custom suicide doors and every bit of the aluminum on it was polished like a mirror.

Behind it was one of their enclosed trailers hooked to one of their trucks that in it-self looked like a show winner. Right then and there I decided I wanted to work for this company. If they had a show truck like the one I was gawking at I knew this was the place for me. I told this to Jim and Max and both agreed that's where I should be. For some unknown reason at the time I could feel my writers block fading away.

While strolling around checking out other cars I spotted a space dedicated to the Cheetah, It was a car built in the 70's or 80's that used a Corvette 427 engine. From the first time I ever laid eyes on one of these I was entranced with them. The lines on this car are unique, it looks like someone took parts of a Cobra, Jag E-type, and a C-3 Corvette then put them into a blender and the Cheetah was the outcome. Talking with the guy representing the booth I learned <u>you</u> could build this Kit Car in your garage using the under pinning's of a C-4 Corvette for a donor car, much the same way that others use a Mustang for a donor while building a Cobra Replica. I got all the literature they had and dreamed of building one. To this day I'd still like to do that but if I were to spend that kind of money doing that why not just get another Vette or find an E-Type I could rebuild. You can always dream right?

We continued looking at cars and went to the basement or lower level and checked out some wild ass rat rides. Some of these were really out there and looked like a real gas to drive.

Leaving the show we went back to Jims, Max took off for Lansing and Jim and I enjoyed a cigar and discussed what we had seen that day. The art that the car builders create with their vision of what goes into making a custom car is astounding. I never tired of looking at and appreciating the art within a car, boat, pipe, and tool or just about anything that someone has created with their hands and mind. Just like a great book the creators put more of themselves into something than most people realize.

The rest of that winter was spent trying to write, Sunday nights Jim and I enjoyed a good smoke and I attended a few meetings of the Lansing Pipe Club. This club as with most pipe clubs had a wide variety of members, all of whom were interesting.

CHAPTER X1

THE ROAD CALLS AGAIN

That summer I did what I said I would do and went to work for Reliable Carrier out of Canton Michigan. Getting hired took longer than I anticipated as I had to wait for an opening and those were few and far between. Some companies have a certain feel to them; this was one of them as the people in the office as well as the drivers were there because they were passionate about what they were doing and truly loved cars. Sure some didn't care so much but for the most part everyone I met there strived to be as professional as could be.

I was assigned to a Peterbuilt made in 2000 that to me looked like a diamond in the rough, it didn't look that great when I got into it but I could see plenty of potential. The first load I got was a load of new Jeep Wranglers going to Lake Tahoe in California for some kind of Jeep Jamboree being held at the lake that year. Besides myself there were five other trucks going there, among them was a driver named David Vesconi, remember I mentioned him earlier. He and I would become good friends as Dave was a pipe smoker too. Now, Mr. Dave takes a little explaining as he comes off as a cantankerous, opinionated, ornery, loud, S.O.B. that has never had a happy day in his life. You must understand that being in the industry we were in on the road this can be a good thing to come off that way as most people give him a wide birth and for good reason. I for one would not want to piss him off any more than he already is. That being said, after getting to know Dave he is one of the most helpful people I have ever met. Three of us left Michigan together heading west. We stopped for diner at the 112 mile post in Illinois at a truck-stop called R Place on I-80, the food there is great and the wait staff always cheerful, which is something that can be in short supply on the road.

After eating, we all jumped in our trucks to hit the road again and I looked over at Dave, he was lighting up a pipe. Well I'll be damned I thought, this ornery bastard might just be human after all. I picked up one of my pipes and gave my horn a blast of air to get his attention and lifted it up to let him know that I too was a pipe smoker. He just gave me an angry scowl, put his truck in gear and pulled out. After we all got back on the interstate I started to give this individual some serious thought. I couldn't remember ever meeting another pipe smoker that was that ornery and pissed off at the world in general. Not being one to pass up an opportunity to mess with someone's head or to yank their chain I just knew without a doubt my new friend and concrete companion would supply me with much entertainment in the future. He was in front of me so after we got up to speed and had traveled for a bit I figured he'd still be smoking his pipe and knowing you can usually judge a person's pipe knowledge by the pipe and tobacco they smoke I was curious so I passed him. Looking over to Dave when I got even with him I checked out his pipe. Oh shit I thought, this dude needs some direction as I guessed, he was smoking a cheap looking pipe and I figured he smoked the same type of tobacco. This I thought could be what is giving him such a dour attitude. I thought just maybe I could help this poor misguided soul out and get him on the road to some sort of tobacco enlightenment, but judging by what I had observed so far this could take some time as Dave didn't seem the type to welcome new things into his being. I wanted to get on the CB and start picking his brain but after some deeper contemplation thought maybe I should gradually ease into the world of premium tobacco and pipes with him.

The three of us ran for another 500 miles then stopped for diner in York, Nebraska, over diner I asked Dave what kind of pipe he smoked and what he put in it. He told me he got his pipes from drug stores and other discount places and that he smoked Half & Half mixed with Sir Walter Raleigh, that's all you smoke I asked, yup he said that's just about all I can get in the places where I get my supplies. Damn I thought this is much worse than I had at first thought. I had enough class to not just blurt out that he was smoking some real shit, I gave him a lot of credit for just smoking a pipe but I knew I would have to educate this driver on the finer points of better quality stuff. Walking back out to our trucks I jumped in mine and rummaged through one of my tobacco boxes and picked out some nice Dunhill and MacBaren tins of natural tobacco and told him to try some of these. We planned on traveling another couple hundred miles that day so I figured that would give him time to try one or two new blends.

After about 50 miles or so Dave came on the radio and actually sounded happy telling me that was some damn good tobacco and actually thanked me for it. Now for a driver like Dave this was a pretty good stretch. We started talking some about tobacco and he was in a much better mood. We still had 15 to 18 hundred miles to go so I had some more time to educate him on the better tobacco that was available out there.

We shut down for the night in North Platte, Nebraska that night we talked some more about pipes and cigars in the truck stop restaurant and found out he liked cigars I gave him some good ones. The next day somewhere around

Cheyanne, Wyoming, Dave's clutch blew out so I and the other driver proceeded on while Dave found a repair shop to work on his rig.

The rest of the way to Lake Tahoe went without any mishaps and the lot of us delivered in fine order. Where we delivered at the lake was defiantly not truck friendly so we all went to Fernley, Nevada to wait on another load or orders from the office telling us where to go next. This gave me the time I needed to get all the way moved into my rig. Moving into one is like moving into a small apartment as you have space but it's at a premium. I spent a day and a half there, then we got orders to go to Beatty, Nevada for the next day to pick-up test vehicles going to Torrance, California. Great I thought I'll be able to stop in and see Marvin Walker the welder of welders. That's just what I did; it was nice visiting with Marvin for a while.

There were about seven trucks that loaded out of Beatty, I was the FNG (F#$$%$# New Guy) so I got stuck with the only car there going to LAX Airport then on to Torrance. Getting that done there wasn't anything for me to load for a day or two so instead of spending that time in Ontario, California at the shit whole truck stop I went to Hesperia, California to Three Sisters and got every bit of aluminum on the truck polished. Then I put a few coats of good wax on the cab and was ready to go.

It took me longer than I had anticipated but I finally got Dave into a better class of pipes and tobacco. This was no easy task I tell you, talk about stubborn, sometimes I thought I could look that word up in the dictionary and would see a picture of Dave next to the word. When I got back into town if I needed to resupply my cigars I always went to see Mary at J.R.'s and picked some up for Dave as he seemed to really enjoy them. I had given him some nice Punch cigars one day, a few days later I called him to find out how he liked them as I was impressed with the way they burned so evenly. Mentioning the burning qualities to Dave he said, well I wouldn't know about that but they sure taste good. Not being all that swift I asked him to explain this to me, wondering why he wouldn't notice the even burn. I EAT them he told me. I was silent for a minute or two trying to digest what I had just been informed of. What do you mean eat them, like you don't light them you just chew on them? Yup he said, the nice smokes you give me will last me quite a long time. I said, damn Dave I knew a guy with a horse named Shea and that horse would eat cigars, maybe you two are related in some other universe and you don't know it. Maybe that explains some of your attitude adjustment issues, I don't mean to be rude but maybe we should explore this possibility, there might be something to it. Dave thought that was funny too as he didn't shoot as strait up as I had anticipated. When he told me he ate cigars instead of smoking them at first a thought about not giving him anymore but after some thought I figured that wouldn't be right as we all enjoy different things in different ways. If Dave enjoyed eating them so be it, who was I to argue with him. Then giving the matter some deeper thought I figured I'd keep him well supplied as I didn't want him eating cheap cigars.

I also met one of our other drivers named Kenny Wencel. He didn't smoke a pipe as much as I did but he did enjoy a good pipe bowl. If Kenny and I would be running together or meeting up at one of our warehouses and shut down we would be in one of our trucks or sitting outside partaking of our pipe and talking about whatever came to mind as Kenny has a vast imagination that knows no bounds. Besides that Kenny is one of the kindest people I have ever met and as you've guessed by now I've met quite a few. He reminds me of my grandfather, in the fact that I have never heard either of them say a bad word about anybody. If we were sitting in a truck stop and someone would ask Kenny for money or something he would give them some and if they needed a shower would take them inside and get them squared away with shower soap, and shampoo then make sure they got something to eat. I watched him do this on numerous occasions, it didn't matter how far gone or in need some of these folks were, Kenny treated them all as if they were a king or a queen. Most drivers I know have preference as to where they travel, not Kenny, as long as he goes someplace he doesn't care, I've never heard him complain about anything. Unlike some drivers I know that would and do bitch about a free lunch. This world would be a much better place if we had more Kenny Wencel's in it. If I was ever in a downer mood on the road I could always without fail call Kenny and be in a better frame of mind in a matter of minutes talking to this kind person.

Getting back to Dave, I guess I'd been working there for seven months or so when I had a weekend off so I went to my storage lockers in Howell to get a few things that would make life on the road a bit easier. While digging through some of my tobacco bins I came across some blend that I had put together many years before that I figured to be aged perfectly by now. I came across the Sherlock Holmes head that held a dozen or so drug store pipes that came with the head, remember I mentioned them earlier? These pipes were in rough shape, I wouldn't even use them for decoration but I thought just maybe Dave might find one or two of them he could use. Rummaging through some of the tobacco I had accumulated in my travels I came upon a box filled with some pipe tobacco that I didn't even think was available any longer. I was in a two bit smoke shop years before and they were going out of business and these boxes of blends such as Holiday, Field & Stream, Carter Hall and the like. I thought at the time that I could make some type of display in a den or smoking room with them as I knew they were old. After stumbling across them again I figured Dave might enjoy them as he leans towards the more economical offerings no matter how much I try to persuade him otherwise. The shop I bought this bunch from was selling them for a buck a piece so I bought everything they had on the shelf that day. This came to about three dozen boxes with the old foil pouches inside. I knew Dave was laid over for the weekend in Canton so I gave him a call telling him I would stop by and drop off some tobacco for him. I pulled into the yard and dropped the tailgate of my pick-up and started pulling different stuff out for Dave to check out.

Once Dave laid eyes on those old pipes he looked as if he had just seen the Holy Grail. In my eyes these things were beyond nasty, not so with Dave, he thought they were the greatest. I gave every one of them to him and he was big time happy. He also became ecstatic over the old tobacco, like myself, he hadn't seen some of those brands in years. I finally gave up on introducing Dave to the better quality blends. Like they say, you can lead a horse to water but you can't make him drink. Whenever I'm out and about and come across basket pipes that I think he might not destroy in a week I'll pick them up for him. Dave is rougher on pipes than anybody I have ever met. I gave him a really nice Canadian I had won that I only smoked a few times. I seen Dave a week later and asked him how he liked smoking it. I don't he said, I dropped it out of my mouth and it hit the ground and shattered. A little note to Dave here, yes that did PISS me off. I soon got over it though.

To this day Dave remains one of my closest friends, whenever I get stuck in my writing I give Dave a call then we both bitch about the world or anything else we can find to complain about then we get on with getting on.

Something I noticed about being back on the road this time was that first, sense we hauled quite a few cars out of the different ports around the country we had to get a clearance card called a TWIC card and you needed to go to certain locations to apply for this card. After applying it took a number of weeks to get it in. They would then contact you then you had to go to where you applied for it to go through more red tape to pick it up. This card allowed the holder to enter sea ports to pick up vehicles shipped in from other countries. All this was OK with me at first but then after entering a few ports I was not even asked for it. Then in other ports besides having the government issued card you had to purchase a separate card for that particular port, on top of that some would charge you additional cash to enter. This was all done in the interest of HOMELAND SEQURITY, I'm all for that but I failed to see where this was doing any good. Seemed like just another bureaucratic pain in my ass.

The second thing that came to my attention was the vast number of drivers on the road that were not from this country. I don't have a problem with anybody trying to make a living, what I do have a problem with is the fact that some of these drivers come from countries that are not exactly our best friends now or ever will be. It seems to me that our so called homeland security is focusing a lot of attention in areas that don't need it so much. I've noticed an increase in certain factions of the work force on the road and these people are getting their own network of truck stops around the country. Watching what is or isn't going on out on our highways and byways has me rather concerned. It sure seems like nobody is paying much attention to what's developing right under the American public's nose and nobody has a clue. When the shit hits the fan then it will be too late as usual. Let's pray that someone wakes up to this threat before that happens and it turns into film at 11:00.

CHAPTER XII

HOW THIS BOOK CAME TO BE

A few years ago Kristie my fiancée bought me a Kindle Fire for Christmas and my life hasn't quite been the same since. In my Peterbuilt I built two shelves that ran the length of the back of my sleeper to keep all my books and movies on as they were taking up too much valuable space in my other storage areas. The shelves I built were seven feet long and would hold quite a few books and movies, then the books started to outgrow my shelf space again and just in the nick of time I got a Kindle. This device was to become my new best friend. What with all the books I read and want to read and things I enjoy looking up this came in handy as I was now able to take a whole library with me wherever I went. Being interested in writing and learning one could self-publish through amazon was beyond cool to me. While I started writing about my 40 years in the trucking industry I really started to enjoy my pipes on a level above what I had in the past. I dug out an old book out of storage by Richard Carleton Hacker titled Pipesmoking A 21st Century Guide. Finishing that, I started shopping on my Kindle for more books about pipes and discovered Rick Newcombe and his books In Search Of Pipe Dreams and Still Searching for Pipe Dreams both of which are very informative. I've always wanted to try my woodworking skills out by making a pipe or two and besides that it would give me an excuse to buy more tools. His books were just what I needed to make that jump.

I then discovered Marc Munroe Dion and his book Mill River Smoke which I enjoyed immensely, then was surprised to find his other book Between Wealth and Welfare, another great book. Marc had his email address in the back of one of his books so I emailed him and actually got a response. I asked him if he was still there and would he consider answering questions about writing and publishing on Kindle. I was walking 10 feet off the ground after Marc answered me back. I immediately called a friend of mine William Carlton that had published his memoirs about working as a beef boner in Detroit's Eastern Market, his book is titled BEEF U. Bill thought I was jerking his chain at first when I told him that Marc returned my email but then came around after he also read Marcs book as Bill is a pipe smoker too.

Another book I found interesting is Old Briar-Pipe Smoking on a Budget by Dave Whitney. I found quite a bit of useful information in his book. Gary B. Schrier's book Confessions of a Pipeman Second Edition is also a very good read for a pipe smoker. I haven't read his book on Calabash Pipes yet but plan to in the near future.

Someday I'd like to just travel around the country in a sailboat, motor home or better yet in a vintage Corvette or an E-type Jag and just visit Pipe Shops, marinas, boatyards, and auto museums only this time I would be on my own time and would stay off the interstates sticking to back roads as I still believe one can still find character in our country if we look for it. Truth-be-told I'd be happy to just jump in my pick-up and take off and go to a few pipe trade shows.

Getting back to pipe books I read both of Rick Newcomb's books twice. I can honestly say that I lost count of how many times I read Marc Dion's books. I follow his columns on the internet as much as I can and never tire of his writing. I hope that someday I can visit him at his favorite smoke shop in Fall River, Massachusetts, and sit with his cronies' in the monkey room (No Member) and see the Christmas Pipe hanging from the wall.

After reading several books about pipes and cigars I thought it might be a good idea to write of my adventures in pipe and cigar smoking as most of what I've read had a lot of facts and figures along with many how to suggestions. I wanted to tell a bit of my story and talk about some of the characters I've come across in my travels. I was going to give my two cents worth of thoughts on different pipe tobaccos and cigars but the only thing in this world that matters is ones individual preference, as long as you enjoy what you pick out, that my friend is all that matters.

Not too long ago I was at a function and was asked to put my pipe out and away, it wasn't even lit and I told this to the ninny that approached me. That does not matter he said, some people do not want to even see a tobacco pipe. Well, why don't you kiss my ass I wanted to tell this little creep, but I refrained from doing so as I didn't want to offend anyone any more than I had by just being there and breathing the same air as the far superior entities around me are breathing. Whenever I watch television I see commercials wanting you to take more medications to jump start the medications people are already taking and then you hear the side effects such as dizziness, swollen hands and feet, improper urination procedures, anal leakage, and a multitude of other side effects. Makes you want to sign right up for that eh. But don't even think about smoking, god forbid if someone was to have a few moments of enjoyment.

A few years ago I finally moved to one of my favorite towns in the whole country. Some call it the Venice of Michigan;

on the map it's called Gibraltar Michigan this is one of the coolest towns I've ever been in as its right at the northwestern tip of Lake Erie and at the mouth of the Detroit River. There are four islands and numerous canals that make up the town. Besides that it's off the beaten path, so if you don't have a boat at one of the marinas or you don't live here nobody comes here. I can walk down the street and smoke a pipe or cigar and people wave at me instead of looking at me as if I just insulted their mother.

Since I moved here I've joined the local Rotary Club and have gotten to know another interesting cast of characters. Most everyone in the club is a boater and has lived in this area for many years. I enjoy listening to their tales of the Great Lakes and getting the scoop on different boats I see around here. I've never had the time or interest in joining a club other than a pipe club but I'm glad I Joined the Gibraltar Rotary. We have one event that's quite well known in these parts and that's The Annual Muskrat Dinner held every March. Tickets for this event sell out quickly. I know what you're thinking muskrats! You're wondering why anyone would want to eat one. In this neck of the woods we refer to them as a Lake Erie Lobster, we even have T-shirts proclaiming this fact. And yes they are tasty.

The one and only thing I don't like about living in the Down River area is that we don't have a proper pipe shop or even a smoke shop that carries decent pipe tobacco. If the pipe men of this area need to replenish their supply of anything pipe related they have to travel a bit north, south, or east, and if they wish to pay more they can always cross the river to Windsor, Ontario. I think it's worth the trip to

J.R.'s in Southfield, Michigan to get a decent deal on pipe tobacco if you live in the Detroit area.

If there is anyone reading this that wishes to or would like to start a pipe club in the downriver area of Michigan please email me and just maybe we can get one started. I will answer all emails.

I'm going to close this book for now and get on with other writing projects I wish to tackle. I've got many adventures to write about and more smoking related ventures that I'd like to share with others. All comments will be appreciated, I can be reached at: dwsenik1@comcast.net

Made in the USA
Charleston, SC
01 March 2014